IDEAS *for* GREAT

Sunset

HOME DECORATING

P9-CLU-098

By the Editors of

Sunset Books

MENLO PARK, CALIFORNIA

Sunset Books

VICE PRESIDENT, GENERAL MANAGER:
Richard A. Smeby

VICE PRESIDENT, EDITORIAL DIRECTOR: Bob Doyle

PRODUCTION DIRECTOR: Lory Day

DIRECTOR OF OPERATIONS: Rosann Sutherland

RETAIL SALES DEVELOPMENT MANAGER: Linda Barker

EXECUTIVE EDITOR: Bridget Biscotti Bradley

ART DIRECTOR: Vasken Guiragossian

SPECIAL SALES: Brad Moses

Staff for this book:

DEVELOPMENTAL EDITOR: Linda J. Selden

EDITOR: Linda Hetzer

BOOK DESIGN: Margo Mooney, www.pinkdesigninc.com

ASSOCIATE EDITOR: Sara Newberry

RESEARCH CONSULTANTS: Scott Atkinson,
Christine Barnes, Cynthia Bix, Barbara J. Braasch,
Christine Olson Gedye, Lisa Stockwell Kessler,
Susan Lang, Don Vandervort

PHOTO DIRECTOR/STYLIST: JoAnn Masaoka Van Atta

PREPRESS COORDINATOR: Danielle Javier

ILLUSTRATIONS: Beverly Bozarth Colgan, with the
exception of page 131, by Eileen Whalen

COLOR PALETTES, COLOR RINGS, AND PAINT DABS:
Christine E. Barnes

Ideas for Great Home Decorating was produced in conjunction
with Roundtable Press, Inc.
Directors: Marsha Melnick, Julie Merberg

10 9 8 7 6 5 4 3 2 1

First printing June 2004

Copyright © 2004 Sunset Publishing Corporation,
Menlo Park, CA 94025. Second edition. All rights reserved,
including the right of reproduction in whole or in part
in any form.

ISBN: 0-376-01259-5
Library of Congress Control Number: 2003115472
Printed in China.

For additional copies of *Ideas for Great Home Decorating* or
any other Sunset book, call 1-800-526-5111 or visit us at
www.sunset.com

COVER: Pale green is a unifying element in this inviting
dining room. Interior design: Sally Weston Architects.
Photography: Brian Vanden Brink. Cover design:
Vasken Guiragossian.

A Fresh Start

When you decide to decorate or redecorate your home, you set out on a quest to give new life to your rooms. Some homeowners are blessed with a clear vision and are confident about the undertaking, while others find the prospect of decorating daunting. Whether you consider the process exciting or intimidating, the steps of the adventure are the same—dream first, consider your options, plan your route, and then set forth with an itinerary that allows a few side trips and a budget that has room for the unexpected.

Ideas for Great Home Decorating will guide you along the decorating journey. Decorating Basics takes a look at the definition of style, the principles of design, and the vocabulary of color, all of which will help you define your perfect decor. The Planning Primer examines the decorating elements common to all rooms—walls, window treatments, flooring, and lighting. Great Ideas takes you on a room-by-room tour, offering hundreds of terrific ideas for making each part of your living space look great and work well.

Throughout the book, you'll find some special features that present wonderful details that add polish, finesse, or fun to a room. They'll encourage you to be creative and go beyond the obvious—and will help you make smart decisions along the way.

So browse through the hundreds of inspiring photographs, pick and choose among the clever concepts and smart solutions used by other homeowners, and feel free to adapt any of these ideas in your home as you embark on your decorating adventure.

Contents

SPECIAL FEATURES

DECORATING BASICS

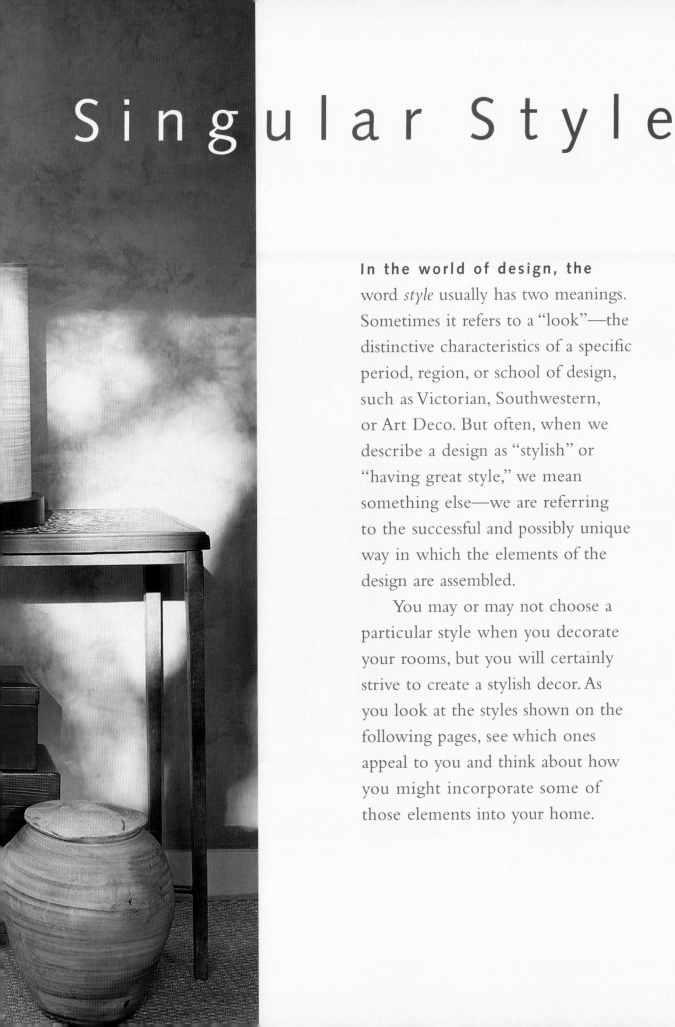

Singular Style

In the world of design, the word *style* usually has two meanings. Sometimes it refers to a "look"—the distinctive characteristics of a specific period, region, or school of design, such as Victorian, Southwestern, or Art Deco. But often, when we describe a design as "stylish" or "having great style," we mean something else—we are referring to the successful and possibly unique way in which the elements of the design are assembled.

You may or may not choose a particular style when you decorate your rooms, but you will certainly strive to create a stylish decor. As you look at the styles shown on the following pages, see which ones appeal to you and think about how you might incorporate some of those elements into your home.

A Way to Express Yourself

Most home decor is eclectic in style, a blend of traditional and contemporary, a mingling of new with the old. The furnishing choices in a successful home decoration are almost always a judicious mix of styles. When beginning to decorate, keep in mind that rarely is a room, outside of one found in a museum, decorated in one style. As you look at the rooms on the following pages, see which furniture, fabrics, and designs appeal to you the most from the variety of styles presented.

True Classics

Classic decor is based on furniture from historic periods. Among the English periods, eighteenth-century Georgian produced furniture styles that live on today in pieces reflecting the sensibility of that era's great cabinetmakers, such as Chippendale, Hepplewhite, Adam, and Sheridan. In French design, Louis XV pieces are characterized by elaborate scrollwork while Louis XVI furniture features neoclassical straight lines and geometric motifs.

Although early American colonists copied English and French styles, three styles that were uniquely American did develop. Early American was a simple, unpretentious style based on European design, but reinterpreted to reflect a more humble lifestyle. The graceful Georgian period in America featured rich hues and scenic wallpapers and is best exemplified by the furnishings of Colonial Williamsburg. The Federal period was inspired by the neoclassical revival; its best-known example is Thomas Jefferson's home, Monticello.

A magnificent antique pine hutch *frames a collection of majolica— glazed earthenware with motifs and colors from nature. Reproduction chairs with a wheat-sheaf design blend beautifully with an antique pine dining table.*

Polished mahogany furniture *(left)*, an intricately patterned rug, and the terra-cotta tile floor all share a similar color in a richly appointed study. The framed prints and sculptural artwork add a personal note to this classic room.

Midnight blue glazed walls *(below)* throw the grand white moldings into prominence in this living room and create a cool backdrop for the white upholstered furnishings. The gold accent pieces, like the ornate frames, and the light wood patterned floor add warmth.

Imaginative use of flea-market finds
(above) and architectural remnants create
a chic country style. The use of distressed
white finishes on the furniture and in
fabrics helps tie together the many
elements in this sunny room.

A combination of family antiques
(right) and comfortable traditional
furniture creates a welcoming feel in
this family room. The floral, plaid, and
striped soft furnishings are harmonious
because they all share the cheerful
blue, yellow, and white color scheme.

An appealingly casual mix of patterns
(opposite) in a soft green and off-white
palette with a few touches of red gives
this living space a comfortable country-
cottage style. In the dining area, a window
seat that wraps around a pine table,
striped Roman shades, and a collection
of ironstone dinnerware displayed on a
plate rail keep the space low-key.

Country Charm

Country decor can take many forms. To some, country is rustic, distressed, or quaint, a return to basics with hand-hewn furniture, stenciled walls, and antique quilts. To others, it is clean and spare, with the purity of Shaker-style furnishings and minimal but distinctive accessories.

A country look can be imported or borrowed from other lifestyles. English country favors floral chintzes and overstuffed chairs; French country features simple pine furniture and colorful Provençal cotton prints. The cottage look of wicker furniture upholstered in sturdy cottons and linens and the garden look with lots of floral prints and lightly covered windows that let in plenty of light both evolved from the decor of summer homes.

Flea-market chic is a country look that utilizes aged furniture that is often redone to suit its new owner. It's a style based on adaptive reuse, such as employing an old trunk as a coffee table.

The continued popularity of country style in all its forms illustrates the enduring charm of a simple, informal way of life.

Traditional Elegance

It's been said that traditional is a style that's always in style. And that is true because traditional is a catchall decorating term encompassing period styles, from many different regions and countries. The term *traditional* does imply certain characteristics though, and those include graceful shapes, a formal look, and a quiet order.

Traditional decorating schemes often use elegant materials like marble floors, formal fabrics, and polished wood, such as mahogany. Accessories may include those made with luxurious materials, like crystal for chandeliers, sterling silver for candlesticks, and rich wood for picture frames.

Traditional decorating schemes are not exact re-creations of period styles; slavishly following one style would create a room that is too artificial looking. Instead, most people choose favorite furniture styles, motifs, colors, and patterns from different eras, creating a mix that is comfortable to live with and one that expresses their own personalities.

A large painting (right) and a mahogany table lit by a handsome chandelier are the focal points in this traditional dining room. The walls, draperies, rug, and upholstered chair seats all share the same soft butterscotch color that serves as a neutral backdrop for the furnishings.

Pattern and texture (opposite top), united by a color scheme of creamy beige with black accents, are the hallmarks of this classic living room. The polished wood floors and paneled walls, together with the floor-length draperies and softly sculptured rug, work together to create an elegant look.

Subtly patterned coral-colored walls (opposite bottom) set off the softly arched windows dressed with classic, floor-length sheers. The mostly off-white furnishings with touches of darker coral allow the windows to be the most dramatic feature in this room.

This columned veranda *(above), filled with antique wicker furniture, has a Victorian sensibility with its exuberant mixing of so many elements—fabrics, furnishings, flowers, and accessories. The richly layered fabrics and elaborate chaise longue give this space the feel of an indoor room.*

A boldly patterned fabric in an intense color *(opposite) used on the walls, in the window treatment, and for the upholstered chair give this dining room an intimate feel whether it is used by day, with sunlight streaming in the windows, or at night by candlelight.*

Victorian at Heart

Although the Victorian era is a historic time period, its decorating style differs from other time periods in its use of abundant fabric, lace, and floral designs to create a mood that is referred to today as romantic.

Furnishings in the Victorian era were characterized by rich fabrics—from cotton to brocade to velvet—used in upholstery, in window treatments, and even on walls. The colors were often deep and intense, like purple, burgundy, dark blue, and forest green, making the rooms dark and intimate.

Although the Victorian age is now regarded by many as excessive and flamboyant, it was responsible for one ever-popular design contribution: chintz. Fields and gardens supplied the motifs—fruits, flowers, leaves, and vines—in colorful patterns. Today many popular chintz designs are available in lighter, brighter colors and motifs, in keeping with a more contemporary sensibility.

Regional Look

Regional styles take their design cues from the colors and forms that are found in their surroundings. The most readily recognizable regional style is probably Southwestern. Its decor is inspired by the deep oranges and golds of its exquisite sunsets, the turquoise of the big sky, and the earth tones of the desert. Natural materials—terra-cotta tiles, flagstone, red brick, and pinewood—are common and harmonize with the native adobe architecture.

French and Spanish influences, combined with the warm climate in the South, led to houses with large rooms, floor-to-ceiling windows, and outdoor living spaces—spacious verandas and balconies. Many Southern homes feature gauzy curtains to let in fresh air, along with furniture covered in large floral fabrics to replicate the gardens usually found right outside.

In New England, the decor may not be identified as a style, but it has many recognizable elements: the use of wood, both in period furniture and in beautifully carved wall paneling; the prominent fireplace; and formal window treatments. The central fireplace and the heavy window treatments, which evolved from simple window coverings, were necessary to ward off the cold.

Today, elements of regional style need not dictate a look, but may simply serve to unify a room's decor and create a harmonious ambience.

The textures and colors of nature *(above)* *abound in this Southwestern living room. The integral-colored adobe walls, the brick fireplace, and the slate floor form a natural backdrop for the suede sofas, rough-hewn coffee table, and oversized sisal rug.*

A spacious veranda *(opposite)*, *a welcome addition to houses in the South, has formal columns and casual Indian slate tile and brick flooring. Distressed wicker furniture is arranged to maximize the view of the nearby pool.*

A Mission-style great room *(above)* has beautiful detailing in the polished wood furniture and cabinets. The chandelier above the dining room table and the lights hanging above the kitchen island are based on an Arts and Crafts design, as are the leaded-glass windows.

Bold patterns and deep colors *(right)*, inspired by the Cubist-like paintings above the sofa, lend an air of sophistication to this living room. The wide stripes on the rug and chair echo the white wood paneling on the walls.

Retro Style

Retro is a celebration of the styles of the past, including Mission style, Art Deco, Fifties—any style that re-creates the aesthetic of a particular period.

Mission style, popular in the early part of the twentieth century, is known for its plain, massive oak furniture, characterized by straight horizontal and vertical lines. Reminiscent of the early Spanish missions in the United States, the designs are pure and simple. The color palette focuses on warm, earth-toned neutrals.

Art Deco, short for *arts décoratifs* (decorative arts), refers to designs of the 1920s to the early 1940s. This design features elegant, streamlined, and angular lines. Furniture arrangements are often asymmetrical, and materials include chrome and other metals, Bakelite, and inlaid wood.

Design from the 1940s and 1950s comprises low-slung furniture with clean lines and fabrics with free-form shapes, often in saturated colors. Materials include tubular steel, aluminum, and laminated plywood. Decoration is achieved through the use of a variety of textures. This period style is simple and functional, combining practicality with elegance.

A vintage tablecloth from the 1930s *was the inspiration for the decor in this sitting room off the kitchen. The floral and striped seersucker slipcovers and the windowpane plaid curtains lend a homespun air to the room, as do the folk art paintings of chickens and the display of antique china.*

Global Infusion

Since colonial times, American design styles have borrowed freely from their European antecedents. Today, with world travel commonplace, decorative elements from a variety of cultures have infiltrated decorating schemes in the most delightful ways.

You can furnish a dining room with a Portuguese rosewood table, place an Indian teak coffee table in the living room, and select Chinese nesting tables as end tables. You can turn fabric for Indian saris into translucent curtains, lay a Mexican area rug as a striking table runner, or hinge Japanese decorated doors to create a dramatic room divider.

The possibilities for incorporating elements from the riches of the world's designers abound and are a great way to add vitality to your decor. Display a collection of Native American pottery, cover a sofa with Thai silk pillows, or line a mantel with Vietnamese celadon candlestick holders. Drape a hand-loomed fabric from Africa on the back of the sofa, keep magazines in a woven basket from Peru, or use an antique Italian marquetry table as a desk. As the world becomes smaller and as you travel, let the designs from different regions and cultures inspire you.

The red lacquer cabinets *(above left) and scenic wallpaper in this dining area evoke the warm, intimate feel of rooms visited on a trip to India. The black marble countertop is the perfect place to display an antique silver coffeepot.*

A dining area *(above right) is decorated with a painted panel from Japan and has glazed walls that resemble antique Japanese silk. A brass chandelier almost as large as the table provides soft lighting.*

The furnishings *(left) were kept deliberately neutral and low-key to highlight the magnificent view in this Asian-style living room. The large mirror over the fireplace, framed in exotic woods and edged with copper, reflects the view.*

An antique screen *(below) forms a serene and shimmering backdrop for the tailored bed and brightly patterned bedding. The eclectic decor of this bedroom is the result of using fabrics and furnishings collected while traveling.*

A bold entry (right) has a pleasingly symmetrical decor. Twin cast-metal lamps with black shades sit atop a half-moon table. The oversized mirror with its graphic frame ties all the elements together.

This large, open room (below) features contemporary pieces in a warm, neutral palette. Accessories are kept to a minimum so the grand piano and the view out the window, the room's focal point, can occupy center stage.

Contemporary Design

Often described as high-tech or minimalist, contemporary design is sleek, strong, and graphic. Generally, it features a meeting of new materials with cutting-edge technology. Glass, chrome, steel, granite, marble, and concrete are commonly used. Open plan designs, where one room flows seamlessly into another, along with abundant light and the absence of clutter, all contribute to a contemporary room's sense of spaciousness and its calming appeal.

Typically, accessories are reduced to the minimum, being selected and placed for striking visual effect. The design sensibility eschews ornamentation, since the aesthetic favors the functional over the decorative.

Contemporary color schemes tend to fall in the neutral range so that artwork or collections may be prominently displayed. Color in fabrics, furniture, and elsewhere may be solid or patterned. Abstract geometric or organic designs are also popular choices.

In this sleek, contemporary kitchen, *a free-form floating island of granite sweeps around twin sinks and a support column, making the column an integral part of the room. The large expanses of wood and granite make the kitchen as striking as it is functional.*

Design Elements

Is it time to rearrange the furniture? Do you want to refresh the look with new upholstery? Or do you want to put together an entirely new decorating scheme for a room? Whether it's a small change or a large one, a look at the elements of design will help you create a room that works for you.

Exploring a few of the concepts that professional designers use all the time—balance, rhythm, emphasis, scale, and harmony—will show you how these intertwining concepts are present, in one form or another, in all successful decorating schemes. Familiarity with these concepts will help you design a room that is exciting to look at, pleasing to be in, and welcoming to family and friends.

A Closer Look

Take a look at the rooms shown on the following pages to see design principles in action. All well-designed rooms exemplify more than one principle because the principles work hand in hand. For example, a room is balanced in part because its elements vary in scale proportionally to their setting and there is a sense of rhythm. When each element is in its place and in harmony with all the other elements, you experience the room as welcoming and livable.

Balance

Balance is achieved in a room when there is a sense of visual equilibrium. To accomplish it, you need to think about the visual weight of the elements. Visual weight is not the actual weight of the objects but rather the perception of their weight. For example, dark, warm, intense colors seem heavier than light, cool, low-intensity colors. Opaque materials appear heavier than transparent or translucent ones. Intricate patterns seem heavier than simpler ones. An overstuffed loveseat appears heavier than a wooden bench of the same size.

In this living room (above), a mix of symmetry and asymmetry creates a balanced look. The furniture is symmetrically placed while all the accessories are asymmetrical. On the coffee table, a visually heavy vase offsets two tall, thin candlesticks. The pillows and throw on the sofa are different yet balanced, as is the grouping of white ceramic vases.

The curtain panels pulled to the side (left) resemble open stage curtains that allow the fireplace to take center stage. The chairs placed symmetrically around the fireplace balance the room and are echoed in the symmetrical arrangement on the mantel.

The brightly colored chaise longues *sitting on a beautifully patterned rug are this room's focal point and nicely balance the row of oversized arched windows. The windows' sheer diffusing screens soften the incoming light and ensure privacy without obscuring the stately architecture of the windows. The use of different occasional tables and the large plant in the corner soften the symmetry of the upholstered pieces.*

There are three types of balance: symmetrical, asymmetrical, and radially symmetrical. Symmetry is having matching items on either side of a central point. Few rooms are completely symmetrical, but elements within a room can be. Imagine a fireplace with identical armchairs on either side, a mirror over the mantel, and candlesticks on either end of the mantel. Symmetrical balance is pleasing to the eye because it is orderly and restful.

Asymmetry is achieving balance with objects of different weights. Imagine the fireplace with two armchairs on one side and a sofa on the other, or the mantel arrayed with framed family photographs on just one end.

Radial symmetry occurs when objects are placed around a center point. A good example is a round coffee table surrounded by curved sofas.

The repeated use of squares and rectangles (right) creates a rhythm in this kitchen. Two different sizes of tile form the backsplash that sits between the long rectangles of the upper cabinets and the wide rectangles of the lower drawers. The symmetrical arrangement of the artwork continues the rhythm of squares into the dining area.

A folding screen (below) made of large, square photograph frames sets the tone in this tailored bedroom. The geometry of squares and rectangles produces a sense of rhythm. The decorative pillows repeat the squares and the soft-fold Roman shade valances repeat the rectangles. The room's color scheme of desert sand, brown, and gray contributes to its harmonious look.

The striped Roman shades (opposite) marching across the top of the French doors create a crisp rhythm in this living room. Repeating the rich color of the walls in the window treatments and in some of the accessories unifies the scheme.

Rhythm

Rhythm in a room serves much the same purpose as rhythm in a song—it's the beat that gets our toes tapping, the design element that creates liveliness in a room. Rhythm is achieved by bringing about a sense of movement in the room. Repetition of objects, colors, shapes, or textures is the most common way to make it happen. Repeating bright blue accents in a pale yellow room by using blue pillows on the sofa, several pieces of blue pottery on a bookshelf, and a blue lamp shade keeps the eye moving around the space and establishes a rhythm.

Repeated elements in a range of sizes, such as framed prints arranged from small to large, also creates rhythm. Curved lines in furniture, architecture, and fabrics, as well as patterns with strong diagonal lines, elicit a sense of movement. The way furniture is arranged can also create a feeling of motion if the eye is led from one area to another.

Variety is necessary for rhythm, too. The repeated elements should share a common trait, such as color or line, for a sense of unity, but they should also be varied enough to create visual interest.

Emphasis

Emphasis is giving more significance or presence to some elements in the design than to others. The focal point in a room can be part of its structure, such as a large stone fireplace or imposing columns. Or the emphasis can be on something you bring to the room—a favorite painting or a large dining table. The focal point can also be a group of objects—a series of framed prints, perhaps, or a collection of glass vases displayed on beautifully lighted shelves. Color can create a focal point as well. A bright, intense color on the walls or used in furnishings gives those elements more emphasis.

When you have chosen a focal point, play it up. If the emphasis in your room is on the large windows with beautiful views, then dress the windows to lead the eye in that direction. If your favorite camelback sofa gets center stage, then upholster it in a sumptuous, intensely colored fabric. Use lighting to enhance your choice of focal point by having a spotlight focused on a family portrait, for example, or by placing downlights above a favorite piece of furniture. Give presence to the focal point.

Of course, as you create emphasis in one area, other areas become less important. If your sofa is the focal point, then the flooring and wall covering should be subordinate. If you want the eye to go to the beautiful stone fireplace, then keep the upholstery less intense. For a room to be appealing, you need to create places for the eye to rest.

A luxuriously large plant *(right) in an equally large planter is the focus in this dramatic dining room. The solid furniture, the color-blocked rug, and the plant are all visually heavy and contrast nicely with the delicate sheer curtains.*

The spotlight is on the round table *(above) in this dining room thanks to a softly rounded, oversized light fixture. The larger-than-usual theme in this room plays out in the oversized checks on the upholstered chairs and in the large mirror reflecting light from the French doors.*

There is no question where the eye goes *(left) in this contemporary living room. The fireplace surround is made of marble tiles, custom-cut and arranged in a bold black-and-white geometric pattern. The furniture and rug in a low-intensity cream color were deliberately chosen so as not to compete with the fireplace.*

The always-appealing color scheme of blue and white *(above) allows for some playful choices of fabric in this sunny room. The large-scale checkered upholstery and the patterned curtain panels with their eye-catching fringe stand out against the cool ceramic tile floor.*

Bold, large-scale accessories *(right) set the tone in this bathroom. The intricately carved and gilded mirror bounces light from the graceful bowed window and reflects it onto the shimmering silk curtains. The mirror's elaborate design reiterates the curvilinear patterns in the architectural capital that supports the sink.*

Scale

Scale is the size of an object or element in relation to other objects in the room. For design purposes, scale is generally labeled as small, medium, or large. A room whose furniture is all upholstered in a small-scale print would lack focus. On the other hand, too many pieces upholstered in large-scale prints might appear overpowering. Large-scale items need small-scale ones for balance, and vice versa. Most rooms look best when objects and furnishings vary in scale.

When considering scale, the size of the room and its structural elements also come into play. A room looks harmonious when objects and patterns are in proportion to one another and to the size of the room. A small room furnished with delicate furniture will have a pleasing look because the scale of the furniture echoes that of the room. A large living room with over-sized windows and a sweeping archway leading to a dining room needs fabrics and furniture that can stand up to the drama of the architecture.

Tall windows and high ceilings *accommodate fabrics with large-scale patterns, such as this multicolored cornucopia print. The window treatments and the large architectural fragments that form the base of the table contrast nicely with the smooth tabletop and the delicate design on the back of the chairs.*

Harmony

Harmony in a room is sensed intuitively. Both unity and variety come into play. Unity means that there are enough similarities in a room's elements to make them look pleasing together, while variety means that there are enough differences in those same elements to create some interest. Too much unity in the elements makes a room boring; too much variety makes a room seem to be in disarray, with nothing for the eye to focus on.

If a neutral color unifies a room, for example, then there needs to be variety in the textures of the materials chosen and in the shape and design of the furnishings used.

When all the elements of design—balance, rhythm, emphasis, and scale—work together seamlessly, then there is harmony in the room. And a harmonious room is one that is inviting, comfortable, and livable; in other words, the best kind of room to be in.

Crackle-glazed paint, gauzy window treatments *with playful ribbon trim, golden-toned woods, and a neutral-colored chair are different enough to be interesting, yet similar enough to look unified. They create a comfortably harmonious look in the room.*

A quiet grouping of furniture (left) decorates a foyer that says "welcome." A moire-covered ottoman slips underneath a marble-topped table, centered underneath a beautifully framed drawing of architectural elements. The variety of accent pieces, all mementos from travels, creates added interest.

A 20-foot-high ceiling (below) gives this casual gathering place a spacious feeling and lets in a great deal of light. The look is carried throughout the inviting space in furnishings as well as surface materials, all in a soothing natural color scheme. The textures are varied—from the soft chenille sofa and smooth ceramic tile flooring to the rough fieldstone wall and pleasing grain of the wood cabinets—yet all work as a whole.

Color Palette

The world is a colorful place.
Wouldn't it be wonderful to bring some of its vitality into your home? You can. With the help of this chapter, you'll begin to see color with fresh eyes. Color is, after all, the most powerful decorating tool at your disposal. With a little knowledge and a sense of adventure, you can transform your home in subtle or dramatic ways.

And mastering color is easier than you think. In the pages that follow, you'll learn the qualities of a color, how colors combine and interact, and how light and space affect color. Decorating materials aren't free, but the magic of color is, and any combination is yours for the asking. Be open to the possibilities.

Colors of a brilliant sun *(above) are the perfect choice for this Southwestern living room with its colored plaster walls and Mexican tile flooring. Blue velvet chairs complement the orange chaise longue, while the chartreuse striped chairs are analogous (see page 54) to the yellow velvet sofa.*

A deep eggplant color *(right) acts as a new neutral against which the yellow and orange stand out. The unusual color scheme, asymmetrical balance, and soft edges of the countertop and chairs combine easily in this offbeat kitchen.*

A small-scale pattern *(opposite), such as the blue and black check on these dining room chairs, can soften the impact of a high-intensity color. Pale yellow walls and cherry wood shelves balance the cool blue.*

Temperature is the warmth or coolness of a color. If you draw an imaginary line on the color ring (on page 44) from red-violet to yellow-green, the colors to the left—yellows, reds, and oranges—seem warm. Warm colors are considered to be "advancing" because they look as though they are coming closer to the viewer. The colors to the right of that imaginary line on the color ring—greens, blues, and violets—are the cool hues. They appear to be farther away, which is why they are called "receding" colors.

Visual temperature is relative; colors appear warm or cool depending on the presence of other colors. In general, the juxtaposition of warm and cool colors in a scheme intensifies each.

Intensity refers to the purity of a color, whether it's bright or dull. Intense colors are the "cartoon colors" usually associated with childhood. Low-intensity colors are quiet and subdued by comparison. A color's intensity is important because, more than value or temperature, it sets the mood in a color scheme. Intense colors are fresh and vivid, while low-intensity colors are quiet and understated. Varying the intensity of the colors in a room brings life to a decorating scheme.

The Pure Color Ring

Most of us may be put off by the standard color wheel because the pure colors on the typical wheel—brilliant orange, pure violet, and bright red—aren't ones that are likely to be used in the home. And the sophisticated, mixed colors in design magazines don't appear on the color wheel.

The color wheel is a powerful decorating tool that shows harmonious color relationships. However, it becomes more useful if you simplify the standard color wheel into a color ring that shows the twelve colors in their pure form only. Refer to this ring as you read about the different kinds of colors and how they are formed.

Primary colors—red, blue, and yellow—make up all other colors. Intense primaries in large quantities can be harsh; low-intensity versions such as cranberry, navy, and gold are more livable.

Secondary colors are formed by combining the primaries. Yellow plus red equals orange; yellow plus blue equals green; red plus blue equals violet (often called purple).

Intermediate colors result from mixing a primary and a secondary that are adjacent on the ring. Red (a primary) and violet (a secondary) combine to make red-violet. There are six intermediate colors on the color ring: yellow-green, blue-green, blue-violet, red-violet, red-orange, and yellow-orange.

You may wonder where brown comes from. Most browns are neutrals. They are mixtures of three primaries and can be dark or light, warm or cool.

Primary, secondary, and intermediate colors in their pure form are relevant because they are the source of all the mixed colors we see. (Most mixed colors also contain one or more of the true neutrals, black, white, and gray, which are not on the color ring.)

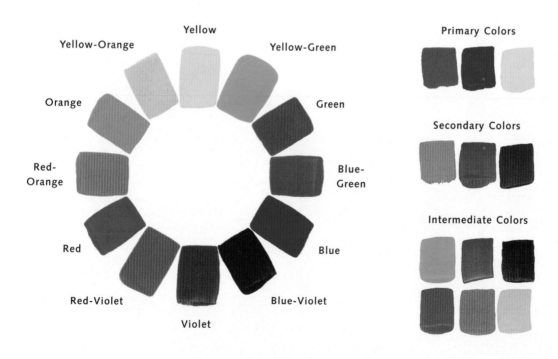

Small splashes of red and yellow (above) create a primary color scheme in this mostly blue baby's room. The high-energy colors are toned down by the slightly less intense blue walls and the light wood furniture.

Glass tile in primary colors plus green (left) decorates this lively children's bathroom. Four colors are in accord when the intensities are similar and all are portrayed in the same small tiles. Larger glass tiles used as drawer pulls add a whimsical note.

The Custom Color Rings

The pure color ring is fine for understanding the origins of colors and their relationships to one another, but inadequate for choosing colors for your home. Color rings that portray the colors in values and intensities you can live with and enjoy are much more useful.

The color rings on this page show the twelve colors in a range of four values—light, medium-light, medium, and dark. All the colors are less intense than the hues on the pure color ring. In reality, you will probably combine colors that vary in value and intensity, which will happen naturally when you use different materials. But the rings can help you become aware of the kinds of colors you prefer and make informed selections.

Light Color Ring

Light-value, low-intensity colors, usually called tints, are often chosen for walls.

Medium-Light Color Ring

Medium-light-value, low-intensity colors are quiet colors with a little more body, and can be used for walls, floors, or furnishings.

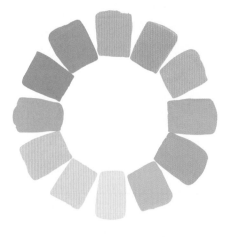

Medium Color Ring

Medium-value, low-intensity colors, versatile and easy on the eye, are often used for large upholstered furnishings because they are not visually obtrusive.

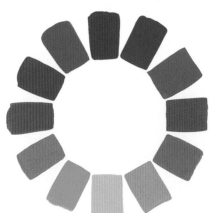

Dark Color Ring

Dark-value, low-intensity colors, which add depth to a scheme, combine naturally with rich woods, especially in rooms used at night.

A small guest bathroom *has a mosaic floor composed of broken tile shards in a variety of colors both pale and intense. The black tile pieces act as an anchor for the many colors, and the solid-color walls offer a respite from the highly patterned floor.*

Complementary pink and green (left) are always pleasing when the colors are similar in value and intensity. This nursery and adjoining study illustrate one of the principles of pattern mixing: vary the pattern, style, and scale, while repeating the colors.

Warm yellow walls and ceiling (below) balance the cool blue cabinets in this high-ceilinged contemporary kitchen. The wood stools, island countertop, and backsplash repeat the tone of the parquet floor.

Many patterns, textures, and finishes *(above)*
give richness to a neutral color scheme of
beige and muted rose, yet the living room is
serene because the colors are similar in value.
The checkerboard rug nicely combines the four
different colors of the furniture.

Walls, furnishings, floor *(right), and even the*
decorative pottery are all a warm, neutral gray,
but each color is slightly different, deftly avoiding
a monotonous look.

Neutrals

The true neutrals—black, white, and gray—do not appear on the color ring, but they do play an essential role in decorating. Sometimes called "noncolors," true neutrals provide visual relief in a scheme with color, without altering the color relationships. Imagine a black leather chair in the company of a red sofa, or soft gray walls as a backdrop for blue furnishings.

True neutrals are stark and sophisticated. In the absence of color, a true-neutral scheme depends on pattern, texture, and finish for visual interest, so a generous mix of materials usually works best.

Just as true neutrals can calm a colorful scheme, color can enliven a true neutral scheme. One spot of intense color in a neutral scheme or repeating small bits of the color in the room can be stunning.

The currently stylish "new neutrals" are low-intensity versions of colors. Put another way, new neutrals are colors that have been neutralized, or neutrals that have been colorized. For example, if you lower the intensity of green as far as you can without losing all color, you end up with a new-neutral green. If you take a true gray, which has no color, and add green, you also end up with a new-neutral green.

New neutrals can vary in value, just like any other colors. These quiet hues are ideal for walls and floors because they are low-key, even when the color is spread over a large area. New-neutral fabrics are a good choice for large furnishings if you prefer quiet colors over strong ones.

Color, pattern, and texture are equal partners in this neutral room. Using materials whose tones vary, even a little, expands this low-key color scheme. Repeating a design element—the geometry of the stripes in the bed curtains, the squares in the rug, and the structure of the bed frame—helps unify the room.

Color Encyclopedia

Yellow

Yellow lifts the spirit and lightens the mood. Soft yellows are ideally suited to walls and furnishings, where stronger colors might overwhelm. Wallpaper and fabric with soft yellow backgrounds are perennial favorites. Pale yellow works with other soft hues while bold yellows and formal golds demand equally intense color companions.

Yellow-Green

Names like chartreuse, apple green, and sage reflect the range of colors in this versatile hue. Intense acid green is a powerful accent, light yellow-green teams with blues and yellows for a summery look, while low-intensity olive and willow harmonize with beige and cream. Pair it with red-violet, its opposite, and it's sophisticated.

Green

If nature has a favorite color, it must be green. Fir, mint, or fern, green looks at home in almost any scheme. It works with warm woods, cools warm colors, and pairs well with blue. Although a secondary color, green is so ubiquitous in decorating it's sometimes called the "fourth primary."

Blue-Green

Clean and refreshing, blue-green combines the calming influence of blue with a bit of the warmth of green. Over large areas, grayed blue-green is easier to live with; intense, tropical versions work best as accents. Historically, greenish turquoise has long been popular for painted wood furniture.

Blue

The color of summer skies and mountain lakes, blue is always fresh and appealing. From cornflower to cobalt to cerulean, bright blues please children, while less intense versions are more sophisticated. The coolest of the cool colors, blue balances warmer hues. And blue and white, a perennial favorite, is simplicity itself.

Blue-Violet

Soft periwinkle, iris, or lavender work in a nursery while intense blue-violet is elegant combined with gold and creamy white. Although considered a cool color, blue-violet is a bit warmer than blue, which may explain its popularity. Pairing it with neighboring hues—violet and red-violet or blue and blue-green—is always pleasing.

Color Encyclopedia

Violet

Violet—better known as purple—has a mixed reputation. Some see it as magical and mysterious, while others find it dark and heavy. Light lilac and lavender are favored for little girls' bedrooms. Violet pairs well with green—visualize violets in bloom. Dark eggplant and grape combine with cream, gray, and black for a formal look.

Red-Violet

Rarely mentioned as a favorite color, red-violet nevertheless appears often in color schemes, usually as an accent or a subordinate color. Most know it not by its color-theory name, but by more descriptive terms: merlot is a dark value of red-violet, orchid is a light value, and fuchsia an intense one.

Red

Bright and brazen, pure red is the hottest, most visually demanding color on the color ring. A red room pulsates with energy, and all eyes are drawn to red furnishings and accents. Intense reds benefit from liberal doses of the true neutrals—black, white, and gray; darker reds, such as cranberry and pomegranate, are quieter.

Red-Orange

More complex than either of its parent colors, red-orange is warm and welcoming. Terra-cotta is perhaps the best known, but coral, salmon, and persimmon are also versions of red-orange. In darker values, red-orange turns to russet, burnt umber, and sienna. Red-orange on the walls envelops a room and flatters guests with its glow.

Orange

Full-strength orange is a brash, bold color that brings to mind fast food and advertising. Few dare to use it "as is," preferring more workable hues like tangerine, pumpkin, and copper. Low-intensity orange is more livable; in fact, most browns are dark-value, low-intensity versions of orange or red-orange.

Yellow-Orange

Richer than yellow but less assertive than orange, yellow-orange is a seldom-used color, yet its luminous, uplifting qualities make it an ideal color for the home. Yellow-orange abounds in nature—think of honey, turmeric, and butternut squash. Blond wood, natural wicker, even brass are examples of yellow-orange in home materials.

Color Combinations

Individual colors are interesting, but the real fun happens when you bring colors together in a room. Color combinations come from classic color theory, and there are endless variations on each. The perfect color combination may be one you haven't yet imagined.

Monochromatic. One-color combinations, called "monochromatic," can be serene and elegant. The key to success with this color scheme is to use materials that are similar in value (lightness or darkness) and intensity (brightness or dullness) with a bit of variation in each. You can create interest in this scheme with true neutrals.

Analogous. These harmonious combinations consist of colors that lie side by side on the color ring. Red, red-orange, and orange are analogous (or related), and so are blue, blue-violet, and violet. The key to an analogous scheme is a common color—red in the first example and blue in the second. An analogous scheme gains interest from a lively mix of patterns and textures.

A monochromatic color scheme *looks most interesting when different materials are used. Here, the smooth mohair upholstery contrasts nicely with the textured plaster walls. A small touch of yellow-green—an "almost opposite" color to violet on the color wheel—in the pillow adds a bit of interest.*

The analogous color scheme *of blue and blue-green with white trim is especially crisp looking. The collection of cream-colored pottery adds a bit of warmth to this cool color combination.*

Complex. Complex schemes consist of colors spaced around the color ring in a variety of arrangements. Teal, magenta, and mango (intense versions of blue-green, red-violet, and yellow-orange) are equidistant on the color ring, in a combination known as a "triad." A four-color combination of equidistant colors, such as green, red, yellow-orange, and blue-violet, is known as a "tetrad." Complex color schemes are pleasing because they automatically balance visual temperature, but they can be more challenging to put together than simpler schemes.

Complementary. Complementary combinations are made up of colors that lie directly opposite each other on the color ring. Red and green are complements, as are yellow-orange and blue-violet. Approximately opposite colors work well, too: for example, sage green (a yellow-green) pairs beautifully with violet. In fact, sometimes it's more interesting when the colors are not direct complements: blue, for example, works well with yellow, a warm color.

Tile in complementary pink and green *(above left) covers every surface, even the inside of the sink, in this fanciful guest bathroom. The green predominates subtly to create a soothing touch.*

In this dining area *(above right), a light-value and low-intensity version of a complex color scheme consists of yellow-orange on the wall on the left, red-violet on the back wall, and blue-green in the background of the rug. The yellow trim ties all the colors together.*

Color and Light

Light powerfully affects the perception of color. A basic understanding of how light influences color can help you make wise color choices.

Most light in the home is artificial, and the color of that light varies. (See Lighting Choices, page 133.)

A room's exposure determines the quality of its natural light. North-facing rooms receive light that tends to be cool, while south-facing rooms get inherently warmer light. To balance the temperature in a room, use warm colors in north-facing rooms and cool colors in south-facing ones. Or enhance the natural temperature of a room with colors of a similar temperature.

The way materials and surfaces reflect light also affects color. A shiny red lacquer table will reflect light and appear brighter, while the same red in a heavily textured fabric will be comparatively dull.

Color and Space

Using color to define or alter space is really about creating illusions. Traditional thinking is that light, cool colors enlarge a space, while dark, warm colors make a room seem smaller. Low-intensity colors are thought to enhance space, while more intense colors contract it. In real life, many factors, such as the amount of light in a room, modulate these visual effects.

Color can be a useful tool to alter the apparent proportions of a room. Painting an end wall in a long, narrow room a warmer, darker color may create the illusion of a better-proportioned room. In a square room, painting one wall a more intense color than the other three walls can diminish the boxy look. Again, many variables can influence these effects.

To create a smooth visual flow from room to room, use the same paint color and flooring throughout. To create a layered look and a sense of separation between rooms, use different colors in adjoining rooms. Or combine both approaches by choosing related but different colors for adjoining rooms.

This antique chest of drawers, *with its vibrant green crackle finish, adds an unexpected note to the decor. With any decorating scheme, consider color on furniture as a way to create interest.*

Sunshine yellow (left) with an almost equal amount of bright white trim wakes up this pantry by the back door. Using large amounts of a warm color raises the temperature of any room and makes it a more welcoming place.

Wood paneling painted a deep blue-green (below) is a cool backdrop for warmer-colored furnishings, flooring, and window treatments. The painted ceiling makes the room cozier, and bamboo shades filter the strong light.

Pattern & Texture

Pattern and texture add interest and dimension to a room much like spices add interest and flavor to a dish. A successful mix of patterns, colors, and textures results in a balanced and beautiful room—the kind of room that makes you feel comfortable the moment you enter it. But it takes a deft hand to create the mix, just as when seasoning food. Too much pattern or texture and the room appears overpowering; too little and the room is bland; the wrong mix leaves a room looking awkward and out of sorts.

So take a look at the mix of pattern and texture on the following pages and learn from the experts' tips how to achieve a balance that will make your rooms as "tasteful" as they are attractive.

The Look and Feel

Pattern and texture bring visual interest and vitality to a room. First look at the patterns and textures that are inherent in the architecture of the room—the pattern in the grain of a wood floor, for example, or the geometry of leaded-glass windows, the texture of plaster walls, or the sheen of a marble countertop. Then think about the patterns and textures you choose to add with fabric, carpet, or wall covering. Soft velvet upholstery, a smooth leather ottoman, and the varied loops of a Berber carpet are textures you may choose to live with, just as flowered curtains or striped wallpaper may be patterns you find appealing.

A Look at Pattern

Patterns vary in design as well as in scale and both play a part in the effect a pattern has in a room.

Style. Patterns come in many different styles. Naturalistic patterns are realistic renderings of natural forms, such as flowers and birds. Stylized patterns simplify natural designs to capture their essence; the fleur-de-lis, for example, is a stylized iris. Geometric designs include stripes, checks, and plaids. Abstract patterns are loose, artistic interpretations of realistic or geometric designs.

Spanish relief tiles in a variety of patterns *(above) are inset in the countertop and used as a single-row backsplash. Smaller tiles frame the mirror. A gold and green color scheme unifies the various patterns.*

The combination of many patterns *(left) might seem overwhelming in theory, but it works beautifully in this room because they all share the same soft color palette. Repeating design elements of large and small checks helps pull it all together.*

A judicious mix of patterns and textures *is pleasing to the eye in this sitting area. Vintage wicker rocking chairs, their cushions upholstered in remnants of old tapestry fabric, flank a new armoire made in the style of 1930s bamboo-and-wood furniture. A table proudly displaying its distressed finish holds a collection of antique quilts.*

Scale. The scale of a pattern is determined by the size of the motifs or designs in it. Small-scale patterns can read as texture rather than pattern and can be a place for the eye to rest when used in rooms with larger patterns. Medium-scale patterns are versatile and seldom overpower other elements. With large-scale patterns, which work well in generously proportioned rooms, make sure you have a large enough area to display several pattern repeats so the design will not look truncated.

It's always best to purchase a yard or more of a fabric, even one that you are immediately drawn to, so that you can see how it looks in your room— close up as well as from a distance, next to furnishings you already have as well as in different lighting conditions.

Architectural details (*above*) *such as the plate rail with its decorative molding and the beadboard wainscoting give textural interest to the wall. The angular outdoor café furniture mixes with the softly curved pine settees, and both are anchored by the richly colored hooked rug. The throw pillows combine vintage floral fabrics with the new stripe on the settee.*

Mixing patterns of various sizes (*opposite*) *helps set the style of this cheery sunroom. The settee's medium-scale leaf print is a perfect counterpoint to the fresh, larger-scale zinnia pattern of the chair, bench, and accent pillows. The delicate patterns of both indoor and outdoor plants contribute another layer of interest, and bold geometric floor tiles add punch.*

Combining Patterns

Thinking about how patterns interact will make the job of choosing and combining patterns easier. And looking at the way professional designers combine patterns with great flair—and often defy any rules while doing so—will offer inspiration. Following are some guidelines that will help when looking at the vast array of pattern choices available to you.

Tie them together. Take as your inspiration the one pattern you are most attracted to. Then choose two more that work with it. Three patterns provide plenty of variety; more than three can be overwhelming.

Use color to unify the patterns. Patterns with light backgrounds will open up a room; ones with dark backgrounds make it more intimate.

Vary them. Choose a variety of styles and use patterns that are different in scale. For example, try a large-scale plaid with a medium-scale abstract leaf pattern and a small-scale stripe that combines the colors from both.

Keep your room in mind. While choosing patterns, think about where they will be placed. Will they create both a sense of movement and a feeling of equilibrium? The medium-scale leaf pattern may be used for the draperies and repeated in the sofa's accent pillows. The small stripe on the sofa may be complemented by the large-scale plaid on the ottoman.

A Look at Texture

Think of the uneven surface of bamboo window shades or a brick wall, or the smooth feel of a polished wood floor or silk draperies. This is what is called "actual" texture. But texture can also be created by sponge-painting a wall or upholstering a chair with a small-scale pattern, creating a play of light and shadow on a flat surface. This type of texture is called "visual." Texture, both actual and visual, gives life to a room.

The brick wall *(right) and matchstick shades provide texture in this room while the striped rug and Asian-inspired pillows add pattern. The solid terra-cotta sofa, echoing the color of the bricks, gives the eye a place to rest.*

A mix of textures *(left) enriches this eat-in kitchen. The decorative tile inset in the granite backsplash, the recessed-panel cabinet doors, the stone floor, and the rattan dining chairs provide interest when set against the solid-color walls and countertops.*

The bedroom walls *(opposite) were colorwashed, then the crevices between sections of the plaster skim coat were accented with a dark glaze to create a subtle texture. The walls provide an interesting backdrop for the silk draperies and tone-on-tone fabric headboard; all are the same color, but each has its own texture or pattern. Bold pillows and a striped chair pick up the black of the bedside desk.*

Texture also affects color. Notice how color on a smooth surface looks lighter than the same color on a textured surface. Cherry red will look darker in a deep-pile carpet than it will on polished cotton slipcovers. The subtle differences in color in different materials is what helps bring interest to a monochromatic room—no two elements exactly match, but they harmonize nicely.

You can also use paint to create texture. Choose flat or matte paint that absorbs light, eggshell or satin with a bit of a sheen, or high-gloss that reflects light, depending on whether you want to call attention to the walls or make them a subtle backdrop for the room's other elements.

Working with Texture

Working different textures into a home decorating scheme is like combining patterns: too much is unsettling but too little results in a dull room. Here are some points to consider.

Build on what you have. Start with the textures in your room's architecture, like a polished wood floor or the rough feel of an exposed brick wall. Add textures that complement one another, as well as ones that contrast. For example, silk draperies complement a polished wood floor, while a textured Berber carpet contrasts with it. The contrast between them may introduce a pleasing difference, one that you're after. In other instances, you may prefer the textures to be more similar.

Use a mix of textures in rooms with monochromatic color schemes or with neutral colors. A variety of textures, both actual and visual, will add overall interest to the room.

Unite the elements with color. Materials with wildly different textures work best together if they are all in the same color range.

The brick wall *(above)* was the inspiration for the earth-toned color palette that unites the dramatically different patterns, textures, and materials in this bathroom. The dark wood of the mirrored armoire provides a counterpoint to the soft sand-colored fish wallpaper, the relief tiles of the countertop, and the stone flooring.

This modern kitchen *(left)* uses large expanses of color to capture attention. The concrete floors and eating island contrast with the shiny stainless-steel countertops while the cabinets show off a variety of woods and finishes.

Large windows *(opposite)* afford a view of the garden while the patterns and textures in the room bring the garden ambience indoors. The natural look of the bamboo blinds, sisal rug, and twig planter on the coffee table complement the fern-print fabric on the sofa.

PLANNING PRIMER

Getting Started

Planning and implementing a decorating scheme for your home, even for one room, is a significant project, but it need not be intimidating if you break it down into manageable steps.

Creating a plan is a process that takes place over time, and not one that ends with a finished product after completing a number of steps, like baking a cake or building a bookshelf. Instead, it's a creative experience that evolves according to the givens in your home (those furnishings, artwork, or architectural features you plan to keep or must work with), your decorating goals, and your color preferences. There are no hard-and-fast rules or must-do sequences for this process, so feel free to follow the steps suggested here in the order that makes the most sense for you, one that will help make the decorating experience easier and more fun.

Decorating Questionnaire

The success of any decorating scheme depends on how well it suits your family—both now and in the future. To create a decor that you will be happy with, think about what you want and also what you don't want. Start by asking yourself "What makes your home your own?" Then, by answering the questions below, and any other questions you may have, you will have a clearer idea of what you would like and how you would like to achieve it.

Before You Begin

Family. You'll want to create a decorating scheme that works for all the members of your family.

- How many people are in your family? Are there children? Elderly?
- How do you and your family use each room?
- Is there enough private space for each member of the family?
- What do your children need? Space for homework? Storage for games and toys? A place to entertain friends?
- Do you and those you live with have the same taste or different taste? Can you blend tastes and possessions?
- Do you have pets? Which rooms can they go into? Are they allowed on the furniture?

Lifestyle. Take a moment to think about how you and your family live in your house and use the various rooms.

- Is your lifestyle casual and comfortable or structured and formal?
- Do you need flexibility—rooms with multiple functions? How many different activities will take place in each room?
- Which room do you use the most?
- Where does your family like to eat? Kitchen, dining room, family room?
- How often do you entertain? In what style? Do you have large parties, intimate dinners, formal dinner parties, informal buffets?
- What are your home-based leisure activities? Reading, sewing, watching television, exercising, playing musical instruments, playing board games?

Assess your space. It's a good idea to know what you have before you begin to change it.

- What do you like about the room you are decorating? What are its assets?

- What are the architectural features of the room? Do you have a fireplace that commands attention? Is the molding interesting? Are there handsome hardwood floors? Is there something you would like to conceal?
- What material does your home have the most of? Wood, stone, metal, fabric, plastic? And what textures dominate?
- How do you use color? What are your opportunities to use more color?

Scale. The size and scope of your decorating project will help determine where you begin.

- Are you planning a new decorating scheme for the entire house? Or will you work in just the living room and dining room for now?
- What are you keeping and what are you changing? Are you keeping the carpet but changing the wall color, for example?
- If your decorating plans include several rooms, how do they relate to one another?

As You Plan

Style. As you begin to pull your design ideas together, think about your preferences and what will work in your home.

- Do you want a traditional, formal decor or something more modern and contemporary? Do you prefer a casual country look? What would look best with the style of your home?
- Do you own a special piece—a family heirloom, an auction find, a favorite fabric, a family portrait, a period sofa—around which you could base a decorating scheme?
- Where do you like to purchase your home furnishings? Home-decorating stores, department stores, furniture stores, mail-order catalogs, estate sales and flea markets?

Color. Color can work wonders—it can change the look of a room and change your feeling about the room.

- Do you have a favorite color? Which colors make you happy?

- What is your least-favorite color? Have you thought about that color in a new form—perhaps apricot rather than orange—used in a small amount as an accent?

- Do colored walls look inviting to you? Do you like the feel of an all-white room? Do you prefer florals or textured solids?

- How would you describe your color preference? Do you like cool blues, greens, and violets? Or warm reds, yellows, and oranges?

- Do you prefer light, airy colors or dark, dramatic ones? Bright colors or quiet colors?

- Where do the colors in your fabrics fall on the color ring? What kind of color combination do they form?

Mood. You can set the mood of a room in lots of ways— with color, with light, with furnishings.

- Do you long for a calm space, or do you hope to create a high-energy room?

- Have you thought about using lighting to add drama to a room?

- What is your favorite room in the house? What items in your house give you a feeling of comfort and serenity?

- What is the one thing on your wish list that you would most like to have?

Practical Considerations

Light. Good lighting is a must and new lighting will enhance any decorating scheme.

- Is your room bathed in natural light, or do you rely mostly on artificial light?

- Do you need more light, or better lighting, for specific tasks?

- Do you spend more daylight hours or more nighttime hours in the room?

- Are you planning to have a flexible lighting scheme to accommodate the various activities that take place in the room?

- Have you investigated what new fixtures, new lightbulbs, and dimmers could do for your room?

- Are you keeping energy-saving tactics in mind as you plan your lighting scheme?

Storage. Storage is always on top of everyone's list and now is the time to plan for what you need.

- Do you have enough storage space?

- What do you need to store? Books, out-of-season clothes, sports equipment?

- Can you create storage areas that will be integrated into the room?

- Do you want to purchase furniture with built-in storage?

Budget. Knowing what you can spend on a project will give you a clearer idea of what you can accomplish.

- What is the most you can or are willing to spend?

- What part of the project can you afford to do now and what can you add later?

- What can you reuse by reupholstering or refinishing?

- Is there furniture you can put to good use somewhere else in the house?

Before the Work Starts

Assess your decorating plan. Take a final look at your plans before you begin any work.

- Is there too much of one thing? Is there a good mix of patterns and textures?

- Is the scheme too subdued or is there too much contrast?

- Is the effect harmonious and balanced?

- Do these colors make you feel good? Are the dark walls a good choice? What about a bright red chair instead of a quiet beige one?

- Will you feel truly at home living in this room?

Gather and Define

Just as a cook needs a recipe and the freshest ingredients, you need a decorating plan and wonderful materials. Gathering those materials and defining what you like can be the most illuminating part of the decorating process.

Create an idea file. Start by looking through decorating books, magazines, and catalogs. Flag photos and ideas that appeal to you, whether it's an entire room, a fabric, or a vase of flowers. Don't try to analyze why you like something; just collect ideas. And include family members in the process because everyone's preferences count.

A wool carpet with a stylized floral design *(right) was the starting point for the decorating scheme in this sunny room. The wall colors—cream over sage-colored wainscoting—were chosen from colors in the rug. The white upholstered chairs and the simple white shades help keep the focus on the rug.*

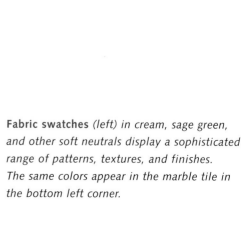

Fabric swatches *(left) in cream, sage green, and other soft neutrals display a sophisticated range of patterns, textures, and finishes. The same colors appear in the marble tile in the bottom left corner.*

Gather materials. Give yourself plenty of time—it will take longer than you think, and your ideas will evolve as you go. Try to avoid the one-thing-at-a-time approach, looking for the right color tile for the floor or a specific fabric for a chair. Rather start everywhere and look at everything. Visit paint stores, fabric stores, furniture stores, department stores, lighting centers, home centers, and interior-design firms—they all hold a wealth of inspiration. Don't be put off by things you don't like. Identifying what you dislike can be as important as discovering what you love. And don't be timid about gathering samples. It's better to consider a dozen fabrics than three;

you can edit later. Your samples might include fabric, paint chips, wallpaper, carpet, wood, stone, and tile.

Use your own starting points. Gathering samples is a great way to begin, but you may already have a place to start. If you have a fabric or rug that you love, list the colors in it and choose other fabrics and paint chips that are compatible (not exact matches) and that look good with it from a distance. If you are starting with a color, consider painting a small piece of molding to carry around with you. Some paint companies have palette cards and brochures that you can work with when you're choosing samples.

Striped sheer Roman shades, *linen accent pillows with fringe, and walls and woodwork all share a pale coffee color but show it off with varying textures and finishes. Monochromatic color schemes always benefit from the use of a variety of materials.*

A Look at Fabric

Browsing through bolts of fabric or stacks of swatches, it's obvious that fabrics come in an astonishing range of choices. You can choose solid or print, smooth or textured, shiny or matte, and your use of the fabric can be minimal or voluminous. Look at the samples shown opposite, clockwise from top left: a cotton chair pad made of chintz and gingham; brocade pillows with luxurious trim; billowing silk curtains; silk and velvet pillows; floral and plaid cotton pillows; and a linen tablecloth and linen-upholstered chair.

Understanding Fabric

Fabric is a material made up of a fiber or a blend of fibers. Cotton, linen, silk, and wool are all natural fibers. Synthetic fibers include acetate, acrylic, nylon, polyester, and rayon. The same fiber, however, can be made into diverse fabrics; for example, cotton can be woven into filmy scrim, crisp chintz, plush velvet, lustrous damask, or stiff canvas.

A pattern can be woven into a fabric or printed onto it. Although some fabrics hold their colors better than others, an absolutely colorfast material does not exist. Bright colors appear to fade more than subdued colors, and solids more than prints.

Most decorator fabrics have a higher thread count (they're more tightly woven) and stand up better over time than garment fabrics. Because they are not preshrunk, and because they are often treated with a finish to resist wrinkles or to add more sheen, they should not be washed.

Choosing Fabric

Consider first a fabric's suitability. Will you use it to upholster the sofa, to hang at the windows, or to create decorative pillows? Is the fabric supple? Does it feel good to the touch and have body without being too heavy or stiff?

When you find a fabric that you like, unroll several yards and stand back several feet to see how it looks from afar. If you're choosing more than one fabric, look at your choices together. Ask for a sample or consider buying ¼ yard of each of your choices to take home and examine in daylight and at night under artificial light.

Once you have decided on a fabric, buy all you need at one time—and, if possible, from one bolt. Before cutting, inspect the fabric for flaws and color differences. If there is not enough fabric on a bolt, ask for a new bolt. If you are ordering from a swatch, check that the fabric on the bolt matches the colors in the swatch.

A Glossary of Natural Fibers

Cotton is stable and durable, resists moths, abrasion, and static, and comes in a wide range of weights, textures, and patterns. It will fade and rot in the sun and can mildew. Untreated, it will wrinkle and shrink during cleaning.

Linen is strong and durable, and resists static, moths, soil, and sun rot. Linen will fade in the sun and will wrinkle unless blended with more stable fibers, such as cotton or polyester. It can also stretch or shrink in humid climates.

Silk is long lasting if handled carefully. It resists abrasion and moths. But it will fade and rot in the sun, and can mildew, wrinkle, and pick up static electricity.

Wool is a durable fiber that is most stable if blended with synthetics. Wool will fade and rot in the sun. It also reacts to humidity and temperature changes, picks up static electricity, pills, and must be treated to resist moths and mildew.

A Glossary of Synthetic Fibers

Acetate is stable and resists moths, mildew, and sun rot; it is does not fade in the sun when solution-dyed. It will wrinkle, is subject to abrasion, and will pick up static electricity.

Acrylic is stable and durable; resists wrinkles, moths, mildew, abrasion, and sun rot; and has insulating qualities. It picks up static electricity and will pill.

Nylon is stable, durable, and resists wrinkles; it has insulating qualities and resists abrasion, mildew, moths, and soil. Nylon fades and eventually rots in the sun. It also picks up static electricity and will pill.

Polyester is stable and durable, does not fade in the sun, and resists wrinkles. It also resists abrasion, mildew, moths, and sun rot. Polyester picks up static electricity and will pill.

Rayon resists moths and has insulating qualities, but it is not stable unless treated. It will rot in the sun, mildew, and wrinkle unless blended with a more stable fiber. It's also subject to abrasion.

Refine and Edit

Now it's time to choose materials and decide where to place them in your room. This step is probably the most exciting, but it can also be the most intimidating. Take it slowly and enjoy the process and the possibilities.

Create a sample board. Spread out your samples on a large surface, such as your dining room table, then pin them to a large bulletin board or piece of foam-core board. You'll see your preferences and your color palette emerge. Plan to leave the samples in the room as long as it takes—that could mean days or weeks. Casually glance at your board every time you pass by; study your samples when you have more time. Encourage family members to do likewise. Don't rush this step—your feelings may change as you see your choices over

A blue and yellow color scheme (right) creates a cheerful-looking great room. The blue chenille sofa and a yellow Provençal-inspired print on the chair establish the palette in the living room while plaid Roman shades and yellow cushions on the stools carry it through to the kitchen.

Simple dots and stripes (left) in related but not matching colors complement a realistic floral pattern. Consider purchasing pieces of fabric large enough to see multiple pattern repeats when deciding if a particular fabric will work in a room.

A collection of 1950s pottery in primary colors (opposite) stored on open shelves becomes the only decoration needed in an open kitchen. The clear, bright colors create the color scheme in the room.

time and under different light. Gather more samples, using your preferences and your palette as guides, if you feel you need more. The gathering process often continues to the very end.

Decide what goes where. Now is the time to envision where your materials will be placed. As much as possible, study your samples where you anticipate using them. Place flooring samples on the floor and put a board painted with your wall color choice next to the wall. Prop up wallpaper books across the room and stand back to see the effect. Drape large pieces of fabric over your furniture. Scrunch up a window-treatment fabric to see how it might appear in gathers or pleats. In other words, let your room "try on" your samples.

Making the leap from trying out your samples to actually buying materials is perhaps the most difficult step in the process. Everyone wants to be happy with the outcome, and no one wants to make a mistake. But if you've come this far, you should have the confidence to go ahead.

Working with a Professional

When a design or decorating job is beyond your scope, don't hesitate to turn to a professional for assistance. Although there will be fees for their services, if you end up with the room of your dreams, the money will have been well spent. Here's a look at various designers and tradespeople.

Architects. For most decorating projects, you will have no need for an architect, but if you are planning a renovation or addition, a state-licensed professional with a degree in architecture may be essential. Architects are trained to create designs that are structurally sound, functional, and aesthetically pleasing. They also know construction materials, can negotiate bids from contractors, and can supervise the actual work. In many communities, you are required to have an architect or engineer sign the working drawings for a structure.

Interior designers. Even if you're working with an architect, you may wish to call on the services of an interior designer. These experts specialize in the decorating and furnishing of rooms and can offer fresh, innovative ideas and advice. Through their contacts, a homeowner has access to materials and products not available at the retail level. They have established relationships with upholstery and drapery workrooms, cabinet shops, and tile, painting, and wallpapering contractors, and can supervise them. Many designers belong to the American Society of Interior Designers (ASID), a professional organization.

Kitchen and bathroom designers. Designers who specialize in planning one or both of these rooms often are individuals who are well informed about the latest trends in furnishings and appliances. Look for a member of the National Kitchen & Bath Association (NKBA), a Certified Kitchen Designer (CKD), or a Certified Bathroom Designer (CBD). Some cabinet showrooms employ certified designers.

Office designers. Some office designers now specialize in home offices. Like interior designers, they understand and have access to the latest materials and products.

Lighting designers. As home design becomes more sophisticated and room usage more purposeful, professionals become more specialized. Lighting designers create a lighting scheme, specify fixtures and their placement, and then work with a contractor or installer to make the scheme a reality.

Media-center specialists. Cabinetmakers, architects, and interior designers are your best resources for designing custom media centers and wall systems. Planning for effective housing of audio and video gear is a specialized art, though, and some electronics retailers have qualified professionals who can work with you and your designer.

General contractors. Contractors specialize in construction, although some also have design skills and experience as well. General contractors may do all the work themselves, or they may hire qualified subcontractors. Contractors order construction materials and see that the job is completed according to contract. They can also secure building permits and arrange for inspections as work progresses. Expect to pay extra if you ask your contractor to design as well as build.

Custom woodcrafters. There are various tradespeople who build shelves and cabinetry. Cabinetmakers create and install kitchen and bathroom units. Custom furniture makers work on difficult, and often expensive, projects. Finish carpenters install trim and cabinetry.

Other specialists. Showroom personnel, furniture-store salespeople, building-center staff, and other retailers can sometimes help create the room that's right for you. In fact, this kind of help may be all you need.

Hiring Tips

Whether you're selecting a designer, a cabinetmaker, or a contractor, start by getting referrals from people you know who have had similar work done. Or you can turn to the Yellow Pages for help. Then call several candidates.

On the telephone, ask initially whether each handles the type of job that you want done and can work within the constraints of your schedule. If so, arrange meetings and ask them to be prepared with references and photos of previous jobs. You may want to visit former clients to check their work firsthand.

For each type of specialist you wish to hire, obtain several bids for comparison. Be sure to discuss your wishes thoroughly first. Ask each candidate for a firm bid, based on exactly the same plans or discussions. You don't have to accept the lowest bid; it's more important to choose a reliable, responsible person whose work you admire, and with whom you feel comfortable.

For some jobs, you may want a written contract, which binds and protects both you and the person you hire. Not just a legal document, a contract also lists the expectations of both parties. When every detail is written down, a contract can help minimize the possibility of misunderstandings later. Look it over carefully before signing.

A large living room has multiple gathering places to serve a variety of activities—*a sofa and chairs around a coffee table, a round table surrounded by comfortable chairs, a grouping of sofa and chairs near the grand piano, and a game table in front of the French doors.*

On the Walls

Walls serve as the backdrop for all the other furnishings in a room, and they can be a key player or a supporting character. You can cover them with color bright or muted, with patterns bold or subtle, with texture soft or rough. You can camouflage or accentuate your architecture, transform the character of the space, or create an intimate retreat.

Choosing the right color is the first decision, and there are many options. Your walls can be bold or subtle, intricate or plain. They can be the star of the show or simply a neutral background for everything else in the room. You can treat all the walls in your home in the same manner, or each room—even each wall within a room—differently. A change in wall coverings is a simple, effective way to refresh your surroundings.

Special Effects with Paint

Walls painted flat colors add style to a decor in a relatively easy manner. But an expanse of solid color may not be what you are looking for. Decorative effects with subtle color variations add depth and life to a room, and many of them are easy and fun to do.

The techniques for decorative painting are numerous and varied. Color washing is a way of applying layers of paint to achieve a rich patina. Sponging, ragging, and combing use household objects to apply or manipulate wet paint. Dragging and stippling utilize dry brushes to create a pattern in the paint. Stenciling and stamping allow you to add graphic patterns to the walls. Faux finishes mimic the look of other materials such as wood, granite, or marble. Trompe l'oeil is painting an object or a scene so realistically that it "tricks the eye," making the viewer believe the object or scene is real.

A distressed green glaze *(above) covers the walls, window frame, and desk in this cozy alcove. The fabric on the chair, with its ikatlike design, echoes the grain of the wood, which shows through the translucent glaze.*

Color-washed walls *(left) in several shades of bronze, which complement the warm woods of an antique chest, provide a rich background for this favorite piece of furniture.*

The choices for decoratively painted walls *are many and each technique helps to set the mood in a room. Clockwise from top left: Blue and silver stamped leaves float casually across a pale blue color-washed wall. A pattern of random arcs and curves created by combing gives this wall a contemporary look. Walls ragged in a pretty pink create a subtle, delicate look. The graining on this door is an interpretation of exotic woods that fit into trompe l'oeil panels, and the faux-stone door frame was created by a combination of marbling and sponging. Soft peach-on-peach color-washed walls sport a stenciled chair rail.*

Wallpaper

It's hard to surpass the versatility of wallpaper. The myriad designs available include traditional stripes, florals, and checks as well as abstracts. The many textures include wallpaper that mimics linen, grass cloth, or other fabrics and embossed designs that look like stucco, plaster, or pressed tin.

Wallpaper is practical, too. It can hide uneven walls or other flaws. It can create an optical illusion—making a room look longer or wider than it is. Or it can provide interest in a room with few furnishings. Many wallpaper styles have coordinating borders to

A nautical theme in this bathroom (above) is carried out with wallpaper that has wavy blue stripes on a sunny yellow background.

A narrow corridor bathroom (above right) is decorated in colors that relate to the bedroom beyond, forming a connection with it. The yellow wallpaper is the same color as the bedroom walls, with a pattern of raindrops; the tile "rug" is the same yellow with a pattern of squares.

neatly finish the room. And with the right choices, wallpaper is washable or scrubbable, making it perfect for kitchens or children's rooms.

How do you choose? Think about the colors you want in the room, the textures you have in fabrics and other furnishings, and the amount of wall space to be covered. Put a sample of the wallpaper you are considering on the wall and live with it in different light conditions and with the other materials you will be using in the room to help you decide if the look is right for you.

Striped wallpaper in two shades of yellow *(above)* on the top half of the walls helps tie together a bedroom decor that includes a mix of Provençal-style fabrics in soft shades of yellow, green, raspberry, and cream, and hand-painted French-style furniture.

Checkered wallpaper that mimics old tiles *(left)* sets the tone in this country kitchen. A quilted valance with tassel trim is an unexpected touch that repeats the red of the wallpaper, and a collection of stoneware dishes in earthy colors completes the look.

Floral wallpaper with a distinctly vintage look *and a fireplace mantel with a distressed finish are brought up-to-date with a jaunty black-and-white gingham chaise longue. The muted colors in the wallpaper allow the wonderful view out the window to stand out.*

Wallpaper Basics

How a room is used will help you determine what wall coverings are most suitable. You might choose an elegant linen or flocked paper for the living room, a durable vinyl for a child's room, and a textured-looking wallpaper that is scrubbable for the kitchen or bath. Before purchasing a large quantity of wallpaper, get a sample or buy one roll and look at it in the room with your other furnishings or samples.

Choosing Wallpaper

Wallpaper varies greatly in its material content, which helps determine how a paper looks and how it handles.

Vinyl wallpapers are popular because they are durable, relatively easy to install, and easy to maintain. There are fabric-backed vinyls, paper-backed vinyls, and ones designed to look like a three-dimensional surface, such as plaster, granite, or grass cloth, which are suitable for walls that aren't perfectly smooth.

Fabric wall coverings are usually made of cotton, linen, or other natural plant fibers, such as grass cloth, hemp, or burlap. Most textiles fray easily and are not washable.

Solid paper wall coverings include hand-screened papers, foils, flocked papers with textured patterns, and murals. Both textile and paper wallpapers should be installed by professionals.

Wallpaper Terms

The back of a wallpaper sample usually contains information on the wallpaper's content, the size of its pattern repeat, and other useful details.

Washable: Can be cleaned with mild soap and water.

Scrubbable: Can be cleaned with a brush and detergent.

Stain resistant: Has been treated so stains can be removed.

Colorfast: Will not fade in sunlight.

Pattern repeat: The distance between the design elements in a pattern.

Prepasted: Back is coated with paste at the factory; only needs water to adhere.

Peelable: Top layer can be peeled off; the backing that remains can be removed with water or papered over.

Strippable: Paper can be peeled off, leaving little or no adhesive.

Run, or dye-lot, number: Number given to each separate printing of a pattern.

Estimating Quantities

Be generous when estimating wallpaper quantities—rolls printed at different times may not provide an exact color match, so be sure to order enough the first time.

Estimating for a room. To determine how much wallpaper to buy, measure the height and width of each wall using a steel tape measure. Round up to the nearest foot. Multiply the height and width of each wall, then add the figures together to get the rough square footage.

Next, measure the room's windows and doors, rounding the numbers down. Deduct these areas from the rough square footage.

To allow for cutting and trimming, figure on 25 usable square feet for each roll as long as the pattern is random or the pattern repeat is less than 4 inches. For a longer pattern repeat, figure on 22 usable square feet per roll.

To determine the number of rolls you need, divide the total square footage of your room by the usable square feet (25 or 22). Round up to a whole number.

Estimating for multiple papers. If you're hanging more than one paper, one above a chair rail and another below, for example, make an estimate for each paper.

Inspecting the Wallpaper

Check that pattern numbers are correct on all the rolls. Every roll should also have the same run number or dye-lot number. Then carefully unroll each roll to check for flaws such as uneven ink, wrinkled edges, or poor color registration. Check that the pattern on the left edge of one roll matches the pattern on the right edge of another. If you find any problems, talk to your dealer right away.

Store wallpaper horizontally in a dry area until you're ready to hang it. Do not place anything heavy on top of the rolls.

Visual texture on the walls *(right) of this modern bathroom was created by a technique called combing. A wide-toothed comb was pulled horizontally, then vertically, through the glaze while it was still wet.*

Real texture on the walls *(below) of this guest bathroom was created by applying colored joint compound with a knife directly onto painted walls, and then a glaze was applied on top of the colored compound.*

Grass cloth–covered walls, *(opposite) a Berber rug, and a silk chaise longue provide a wide range of textures, all in the same shade of heavy cream, in this monochromatic living room. The variety of textures used illustrates just how elegant a monochromatic color scheme can be.*

Texture on the Walls

Texture on the walls lends warmth to a room and also literally brings another dimension to it. Texture can be accomplished in many ways, from simply covering the walls with fabric or a textured wallpaper to adding great depth with thickly applied plaster.

Walls can have real texture, the kind you can feel when you touch the walls, or visual texture, where a patterned surface looks dimensional through the play of light and shadow. Either kind of texture adds richness to a room.

Many walls have an inherent texture. Think of brick walls, wood paneling, beadboard, widely grouted ceramic tile, glass mosaic tile, and concrete. If one or more of the walls in a room already has a textured surface, you can incorporate it into your decorating scheme. You can play up the texture or minimize it depending on the furnishings and accessories you choose and how the lighting plays off the textured surfaces.

Warm wood paneling (above) in a rich natural redwood creates a welcoming look in this tiny dining area that adjoins the living room and connects to the kitchen through French windows, which are often left open.

Wainscoting of ceramic tile (right), topped with a border of tile, is an unusual touch in this country-style dining room. Tile of the same color is inset in the floor to create a "rug" beneath the dining table.

More Options

When it comes to wall-covering choices, you may want to think outside the box, as they say, and consider new materials as well as traditional materials used in new and different ways.

So think beyond paint and wallpaper, and explore the possibility of stone, ceramic tile, wood, and metal. You can use these materials to cover one wall, the upper or lower portion of all four walls, or as an accent in combination with a traditional wall covering. Think about new places to use them, such as decorative tile in the dining room or wood in the bathroom.

To decide whether a particular material is appropriate, take into consideration where in the house the room is located, how the room is used, and how easy or difficult it will be to maintain the material.

Tightly abutted cork tiles in a muted gray *(above left) create a soft, neutral background for the modern furniture and large, black-and-white photos.*

Copper tiles, glass blocks, and ceramic tiles *(left) in a graphic arrangement are a surprising mix of materials for a living room wall. The furniture and carpet in shades of white are deliberately kept subdued in order to give this wall its due.*

Window Treatments

Windows not only let light
and air into our homes, they expand
the sense of interior spaciousness
while they frame our view of the
world beyond. Windows are nothing
short of wonderful. But for all their
benefits, windows present more
than a few aesthetic and practical
challenges. Uncovered, they admit
harsh sunlight, passing glances, and
chilling drafts. Bare windows can
also appear cold and unfinished. For
both beauty and function, most
windows need window treatments.

Your window-treatment options
are many. On the following pages,
you will see familiar styles and old
favorites with fresh interpretations.
But also take a look at what's new
and innovative in window dressing.
There's no doubt that the choices
for windows follow the trends and
fashions in home decor. With a little
planning, you can find just the right
treatment and add your windows to
the best-dressed list.

Dressed for Success

Graceful swags, relaxed panels, hardworking blinds—behind every winning window treatment is a careful plan, one that suits both the design of the window and the style of your home. Start with an overview of style possibilities, then think about color and design. And don't forget the great new choices in hardware. Functional matters like privacy and light control are important, too. Some windows are easy to handle; others are a real challenge. But for each one, there's a variety of pleasing and practical choices.

Curtains and Draperies

Both curtains and draperies consist of panels of fabric; it is how they are attached at the top that determines which category they fall into.

By definition, curtains are gathered on a rod or attached to a rod by tabs, ties, or rings. If the curtains open and close, it is by hand. Full-length curtains can be either elegant or informal. Voluminous curtains that puddle on the floor look luxurious; simple curtains tied back above the sash look casual. Flat panel curtains have little or no fullness. Café curtains cover only the lower half of the window, ending at the sill. Pleated curtains are pleated panels attached to rings or clips. (They can easily be confused with pleated draperies attached by rings to decorative traverse rods because they look alike. The difference is in how they are operated.) Curtains combine well with other treatments: miniblinds or a pleated shade for privacy, topped with a cornice or valance for a more finished look.

Traditional pinch-pleated draperies *operate easily on a traverse rod and retain their pleats for a crisp look. Sheer curtains underneath help diffuse the light in this classic dining room.*

Pleated sheer curtains hung on a thin rod *feature a wide band of brown silk near the lower edge; a narrow band of silk placed high repeats the color and accentuates the lines of the clerestory window.*

Once the mainstay of window fashions, the pinch-pleated drapery has evolved into a collection of designs with imaginative and innovative pleats. As with curtains, the heading sets the style and mood. Draperies are pleated panels hanging from hooks that attach to small slides on a standard or decorative traverse rod. You open and close the panels by a cord that moves the slides along a track. A standard traverse rod is covered by the top of the pleated panels while a decorative traverse rod is always exposed.

Pinch pleats, the traditional drapery heading, consist of three shallow folds tacked at the base. Variations on this basic style include goblet, a sophisticated pleat that forms a cylinder; reverse, with the pleats folded to the back; fan, with pleats tacked at the top only to form a cascade; and butterfly, made with two pleats. Another style, pencil pleats, is formed with the use of pleating tape sewn to the back of the heading. You gather the heading into narrow pleats by pulling cords inside the tape.

Deeply scalloped valances in a floral-and-stripe print, *mounted just below the crown molding,*
are paired with matching side panels in a sunny bedroom. A tassel fringe accentuates the dramatic
scallop while plaid lining in the same color scheme peeks out from the edges of the panels.

Practical Matters

Window treatments do much more than just adorn windows; they are also practical. To best meet your needs, consider the myriad functions of window treatments.

Light control. The primary function of a window is to provide natural light. How much light enters the room depends on the number of windows—their size, shape, and orientation—and the window treatments. To admit maximum light, choose treatments that clear the glass when opened or raised. To filter light and control glare, think about sheer panels, blinds, or translucent shades. To block light, consider treatments lined with blackout linings. Blinds of all kinds, when tilted, block most of the light.

Climate control. To take advantage of refreshing breezes, choose window treatments that completely clear the window; stationary panels or deep valances that cover part of the glass will block the flow of air.

Privacy. Sheer and translucent treatments provide some daytime privacy while allowing light to enter. To ensure total privacy at night, when homes are lit, you will need a heavier window treatment that closes completely.

Noise control. Window treatments can reduce noise from both outside and inside the house. In general, the softer and more generous the treatment, the more sound it will absorb.

View. When the view deserves to be seen, choose a treatment that clears the glass completely and one that blends with the walls to focus attention on the outdoors. If the view is unattractive, choose a white or light-colored treatment that admits light when lowered or closed—and keep it that way. Shutters with narrow louvers and micro-miniblinds are both effective at blocking the view, even to some extent when tilted open.

Safety. If you have young children or pets, window-treatment safety is a concern. Consider cordless horizontal blinds or cellular shades. On two-cord shades, cut the cords and add a separate tassel to the end of each cord. For continuous-loop systems, install a permanent tie-down device or cleat to the wall or replace looped cords with a wand.

Simple cotton draperies *in a fruit-and-plant motif edged with a band of solid-color linen are placed on top of bamboo blinds. Pineapple finials on the curtain rods continue the tropical theme.*

Shades

Among the most practical window treatments, shades can be just as decorative as they are hardworking. Options are versatile and varied, and include simple roller shades; insulated honeycomb shades; woven shades made of reeds, grasses, or thin strips of wood; and soft fabric shades.

Fabric shades—Roman, balloon, and cloud—raise and lower by means of cords threaded through rings sewn into the back of the shades. Shades work well in the following situations: when your window doesn't allow for full, fabric-rich treatments; when you have corner windows without much space between; when you want an uncluttered look; when you want to use a minimum of fabric; or when you want to feature fabric with prominent motifs or a large repeat.

With almost any shade, you can choose an inside or outside mount. A shade mounted inside fits neatly within the window opening, making it ideal for windows with handsome frames. An outside-mounted shade is attached above the window, on the frame or wall, and covers the frame or extends beyond at the sides and bottom when lowered. It's the preferred mount if you want maximum light control and insulation, or if you want to stack the treatment completely off the glass.

A soft Roman shade in burlap *adds texture to this kitchen corner. The neutral color of the walls and window shade keep the focus on the antique quilt.*

A short, swagged Roman shade *(above)* in ivory lace adorns a bedroom window where privacy is not an issue. A smaller, one-scallop version of the shade is just right for a tiny corner window. Mocha-colored trim on the shades unites the window treatments and coordinates with the room's color scheme.

Cloud shades in celadon silk *(left)* dress a recessed window and the window beside it in quiet, elegant style. Thick welting, knotted at the ends, finishes the upper edges, and a tasseled fringe enlivens the bottom edges.

Measuring Windows

To estimate the amount of fabric you need for a window treatment, or to order window treatments from a mail-order source, you will need to measure your windows. The best approach, the one used by professionals, is to work directly from the window measurement rather than from the hardware.

For accuracy in measuring, use a steel tape measure.

For a treatment mounted inside the window, measure the width of the opening (**A**) and the length (**B**).

If your treatment will hang outside the window opening, as most do, you'll also have to measure the area to be covered to the left (**C**) and right (**D**) of the opening, and the distance above the opening (**E**). The top of the treatment is usually even with the top of the trim board, but you may also mount a treatment just below the ceiling, at the bottom of the crown molding, or halfway between the ceiling and the window opening.

The distance below the opening (**F**) varies, depending on the treatment style. Some treatments end at the windowsill. Apron-length treatments usually end 4 inches below the opening. Floor-length treatments usually end ¼ to 1 inch from the floor, but if you want the panels to puddle on the floor, allow several inches extra when measuring.

A flat Roman shade is fitted to this curved window.
Subtle striped wallpaper provides a muted backdrop for the floral fabric shade, the framed flower prints that flank the window, and the embroidered pillow shams.

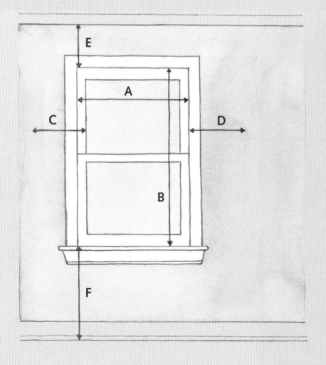

A Window width
B Window length
C Left extension
D Right extension
E Distance above
F Distance below

Blinds and Shutters

Blinds and shutters have adjustable louvers and vanes that can be tilted to filter the light, leveled to reveal the view, or shifted to completely block it.

Blinds, both functional and decorative, can be used on their own (many have optional self-valances) or under top treatments made of fabric. Horizontal blinds, made of metal or vinyl, come in a wide array of finishes and colors. Metal blinds are available in three sizes: micro (½- or ⅝-inch slats), mini (1-inch slats), and Venetian (2-inch slats). Wood blinds mimic the look of shutters at a much lower cost. Painted or stained, the slat sizes range from 1 to 3 inches.

Vertical blinds tend to create a more contemporary look, and come in a variety of textures and materials, most often fabric and vinyl.

Shutters add architectural interest and drama to a window. Available in wood and vinyl, traditional shutters have 1¼-inch louvers that provide privacy but cut down on light and often block the view. Plantation shutters have wider louvers, 2½-inch and 3½-inch sizes, that allow better ventilation and a clearer view.

Subtly grained wood blinds *with 2-inch slats and decorative cloth tape coordinate with the wide wood trim on this triple window. The result is a simple treatment that is as attractive as it is functional.*

Traditional shutters *are an important architectural feature in this room as well as the window treatment of choice. The stained wood shutters unify the large and small windows and reinforce the tailored decor of this room.*

Top Treatments

Top treatments provide the crowning glory for a window. You can use them alone to accent an uncovered window or combine them with other window coverings.

Valances. Today's valances are among the most imaginative and versatile of window decor. They are typically paired with shades or blinds, combining the softness of fabric with the practicality of a hardworking treatment. Many valances are simply shortened versions of curtains, draperies, or fabric shades. Standard valance length is 12 to 18 inches at the center; shaped valances are longer on the sides. Used alone, valances bring a bit of style to a window. Placed over another treatment, they conceal the heading and add a decorative flourish. The lower edge of a valance provides an opportunity for trimming of all kinds.

Cornices. Because their edges are so clearly delineated, cornices add architectural interest. Wood cornices mimic the look of deep crown molding; upholstered cornices give a room a softer look. A straight lower edge is simple and tailored, while a scalloped one is more formal. And cornices serve two practical purposes: they cover the heading and hardware of the undertreatment, and block any drafts.

A cloud valance in blue gingham, *shirred at the heading and ruffled at the lower edge, is an imaginative treatment for a girl's room.*

Gently curved, fabric-covered cornices *are a crisp top treatment for vertical blinds. The blinds provide complete privacy while filtering the light. The cornice fabric is repeated in the pillows on the sofa.*

Swags and cascades. Among the most impressive of all window treatments, swags and cascades bring distinction and classic form to windows. Once found only in opulent settings, today's versions are more casual and adapt to informal decorating schemes. Traditional swags look like flowing lengths of fabric and are challenging to make and mount, while running swags are easy to wrap around a pole or drape on swag holders.

A simple swag (above) in a fresh floral fabric is lined with a perky gingham—both fabrics are used elsewhere in the room. The swag frames a handsome window that looks out into the garden and lets in light while revealing the view.

Silk cutout swags with full-length side panels (right) soften tall windows but do not obscure their beauty. The café au lait color of these swags repeats the color of the walls, carpet, and sofa.

Window Wear

Ideas for great window treatments are both plentiful and varied, sometimes to the point of pleasant confusion. Rather than focusing on the coverings, why not start with the windows? The more thought you give to their attributes (and limitations), the easier it will be to determine which treatments work best on which windows. Here you'll find ten window styles and suggestions for various treatments.

Alcove. A window that sits in an alcove is often difficult to dress because there is limited or sometimes no space around the window. A simple treatment with minimal hardware is the way to go. Opposite, a tapered valance frames the view and a built-in seat is the place to enjoy it.

Awning. Awning windows are hinged and swing outward, usually in combination with fixed-glass windows, with the awning portion at the top or bottom. Choose treatments that cover the fixed portion but do not block the awning window, and avoid any treatment that may interfere with the handles. Consider a Roman shade that pulls up easily to allow access to the window.

Bay or bow. A bay is a recessed window with angled sections; a bow has windows set in a gentle curve. If the view is great and privacy and light control are not concerns, this is a wonderful window to leave uncovered. Or allow handsome window frames to show by using inside-mounted café curtains or shades. On closely spaced windows, add a continuous valance. Opposite, café curtains are topped with a series of shallow swags and cascades.

Casement. Hung singly or in pairs, casement windows have sashes that are hinged on the side and crank or push outward. Blinds and shades are appropriate, especially softened with a valance or cornice. Try curtains on tabs that clear the glass completely when stacked back and allow in maximum light and ventilation.

Corner. Windows in a corner can be treated as one or have simple, matching treatments. In general, do not use treatments with fullness in the corner to avoid a cluttered look. Opposite, the windows have matching swags and sill-length cascades on the outer sides only for a clean look.

Double-hung. Popular windows appreciated for their graceful proportions and hardworking features, double-hung windows have two sashes—an upper, outside sash that moves down and a lower, inside sash that moves up. Double-hung windows allow for almost any window treatment. For a look that completely covers the window, try pleated curtain panels on rings on top of wood blinds. For a more casual look, opposite, try a London shade mounted inside the window frame.

French doors. Elegant and graceful, French doors consist of a pair of glass-paneled doors, one or both of which open. For outward-swinging doors, almost any treatment is appropriate. For inward-swinging doors, the treatment must clear the door frame or be attached to the doors themselves. Opposite, patterned sheers on rings are attached to a wire cable.

Picture. Used in combination with sliding or casement windows, picture windows (also called fixed-glass windows) let in plenty of light and frame the view. Choose a treatment that is in keeping with the size and proportion of the window. When operable windows flank a fixed window, it's important to select a treatment that stacks back completely. For a formal look, opposite, a box-pleated valance tops the draperies.

Sliding. Sliding windows and doors are utilitarian, so easy operation should be a primary factor in choosing a treatment. Draperies on one-way traverse rods or vertical blinds that stack back are good choices for sliding doors. For windows, blinds or pleated shades work well. Opposite, soft Roman shades are topped with a shaped valance.

Triple. Windows with multiple panels may seem hard to dress at first, but using a treatment that considers the windows as one opens up many possibilities. Opposite, a simple cutout swag—with the same number of loops as window panels—is finished with cascades at the sides.

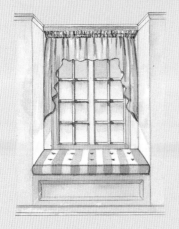

Alcove

Awning

Bay

Casement

Corner

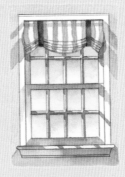

Double-hung

French doors

Picture

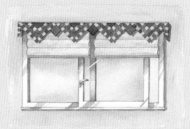

Sliding

Triple

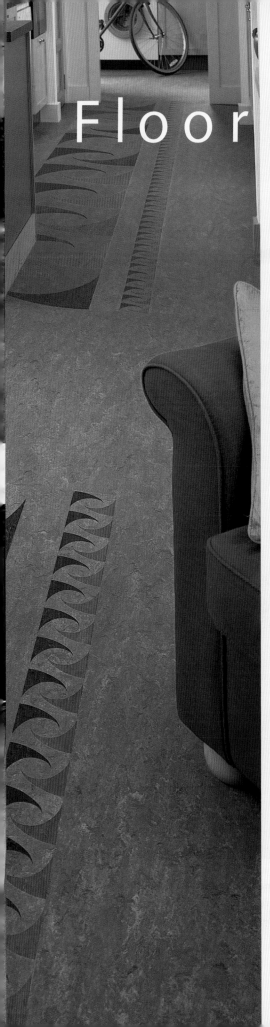

Flooring Options

There is a new attitude toward flooring materials. It no longer has to be tile in the kitchen and wood in the living room. There are new materials and new ways to use traditional materials. What remains true is that you want your floor to be as beautiful as it is hardworking.

Since the floor is the next largest surface in a room after the walls, you'll want to give it the same careful attention that you give any other design element. Think first about your options—stone, tile, wood, resilient, carpet, laminate, even concrete. You'll find that each type of material is rich in color, texture, and pattern in addition to being suitable for different uses throughout your home.

Choose a light-color floor that exudes spaciousness or a dark floor that anchors a room's furnishings. Opt for a boldly patterned floor or highlight a special feature. Whatever you choose, it should complement the design of your room and meet your practical needs.

Ceramic and Stone Tile

Tile is appealing and multifaceted. It consists of ceramic flooring pavers, terra-cotta, and charming mosaics in all shapes and sizes, as well as new products like metal tiles, photographic tiles, glass tiles, and porcelain pavers. Flooring tile, in contrast to wall tile, has a low water absorption rate and dense body making it strong enough

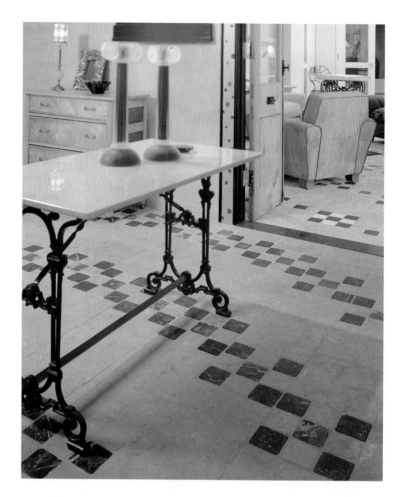

to walk on. Some floors feature the timeless look of tile set with wide grout lines; others with tight-fitting joints look seamless.

Stone tiles can be finished to be smooth as glass or tumbled for a timeworn appearance. Each type of natural stone, from marble and limestone to granite and slate, features a unique color, pattern, and hardness. Stone is more costly than other tile. If cost is a factor, you'll want to use it where it has the most impact—in a foyer, for instance, to make a great first impression.

An intricate floral-pattern "rug" (above) of mosaic tiles is set into diagonally-placed limestone tiles in the floor of this dining room. The limestone tiles the color of beach sand allow the rich earth-toned colors in the "rug" to predominate.

The flooring in this foyer (above right) combines large honed-marble squares with a grid of smaller tumbled-marble squares laid in a gentle arc to direct guests inside. A polished marble tabletop on a wrought-iron base completes the look.

Mixed neutral shades (left) of desert slate tiles run right up to the wood wainscoting in a den, continuing the room's refined Mission style. The tiles were set with tight joints for a nearly seamless look.

Set on an angle (below) with traditional grout lines, pale gray ceramic tile covers the floor of a kitchen and dining area. The lines of the floor draw the eye to the doors that lead to an outdoor patio.

In an open kitchen (right), patterned sheet vinyl looks like individually laid tiles. This floor's neutral tones are in keeping with the room's decor, and its design adds visual texture to the white-columned space.

Vinyl sheet flooring in a mosaic pattern (below) that evokes garden paths of long ago brings the outdoors into a sunny family room. Wicker furniture and potted plants further the outdoor decor.

Resilient Flooring

Resilient flooring is a material you can have fun with. Relatively inexpensive, easy to install, and simple to maintain, it invites playful design. Although vinyl comes first to mind, resilient flooring encompasses a range of malleable materials—vinyl, linoleum, cork, and rubber—each with its own unique characteristics. Linoleum, which is now enjoying a resurgence, can take on a retro look. Cork adds a touch of nature while helping to mute sound in a media room or in a playroom.

Rubber flooring has a contemporary look and holds up to rugged use—a good choice in a kitchen or mudroom.

It's a given that all resilient flooring is comfortable underfoot and performs well in hardworking areas, such as kitchens and laundry rooms. But since resilients are also available in the broadest spectrum of colors of any flooring material, and in surprisingly authentic-looking patterns, like stone designs and wood-patterned vinyls, they are suitable for other rooms in the house as well.

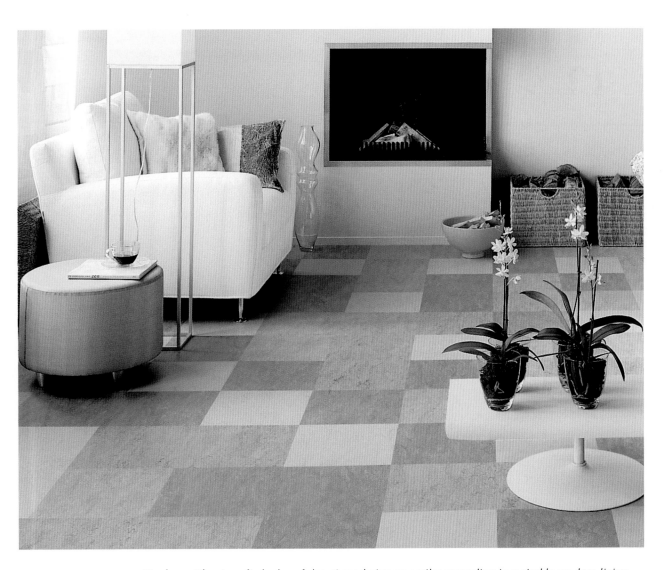

Linoleum tiles *in soft shades of desert sand give an earthy grounding to a starkly modern living room. Baskets for firewood and plants on the coffee table pick up the natural feel of the floor and soften the look of the white furnishings.*

Laminate Flooring

Laminate, one of the newest types of flooring, is a high-pressure melamine that consists of a base of several layers of paper impregnated with resins. A top layer of decorative paper determines the design, which means if something can be photographed, it can be laminated. Introduced in Sweden as an alternative to hardwood floors, laminate combines goods looks, easy maintenance, and quick installation.

Golden bamboo laminate flooring *(above) captures the global decor of a family room while providing a neutral background for the room's exotic, dark-toned furnishings.*

A laminate floor *(top) emulates a ceramic tile surface in this old-fashioned bathroom. The modular tile units fit together along simulated "grout lines," giving the look of a traditional tile floor.*

Most laminates replicate wood flooring and come in a range of styles—from elegant to rustic to contemporary, and include precious and exotic woods, like chestnut or teak, and intricate and sophisticated designs, such as weaves and herringbones.

In addition to wood, laminate tiles in ceramic and stone patterns are also available. Cut into squares rather than planks, these laminates allow for some creative applications. They can also be produced to look like marble and granite.

A wall of handsome turquoise cabinets (above) is anchored by a light pine laminate floor. The pattern of the narrow planks runs parallel to a main wall, visually expanding the kitchen's width.

A minimalist bedroom (right) receives its visual interest from an artfully laid laminate floor that resembles ceramic tile. The simple lines of the furniture and the soft neutral colors of the furnishings reflect the floor's muted shades.

A **contemporary wool rug** *(right)* in neutral shades of cocoa and gray makes a bold statement in this great room. The oversized square coffee table repeats the large squares in the rug.

A **natural-color loop pile Berber carpet** *(below)* harmonizes with the nubby texture of the sofa in this living room, providing a neutral background for the dark coffee table with its beautifully curved legs.

Carpet

There's no denying the warmth and security that a carpet brings to a room. It also provides comfort underfoot. New technologies have allowed for greater texture and surface interest in carpet, as well as multiple colors and overall patterns. Loop styles include level loop, multilevel loop, cut pile, and cut-and-loop combinations. In addition, designs can be sculpted so they appear to pop out. Synthetic fibers have become more pleasant to the touch. And carpets made of woven plants and grasses, such as sisal, are now more versatile. Today's stain-resistant finishes mean easy care and less worry.

You can choose area rugs or wall-to-wall carpeting. Area rugs work well when you want an existing wood floor to remain visible. Or you can use a rug to delineate one area of a floor, like a dining space. In a bedroom suite, you may prefer wall-to-wall carpeting with its cushioning comfort and ability to absorb sound.

An allover Persian-inspired center pattern *and an intricate floral border are the hallmarks of this Oriental rug. Not only does the carpet provide a design focus in the foyer, it also protects the wide plank hardwood floors.*

A contemporary abstract-patterned rug *contrasts nicely with the texture of the chenille-covered easy chair and the leather ottoman, but all the elements are compatible because they share a palette of related colors.*

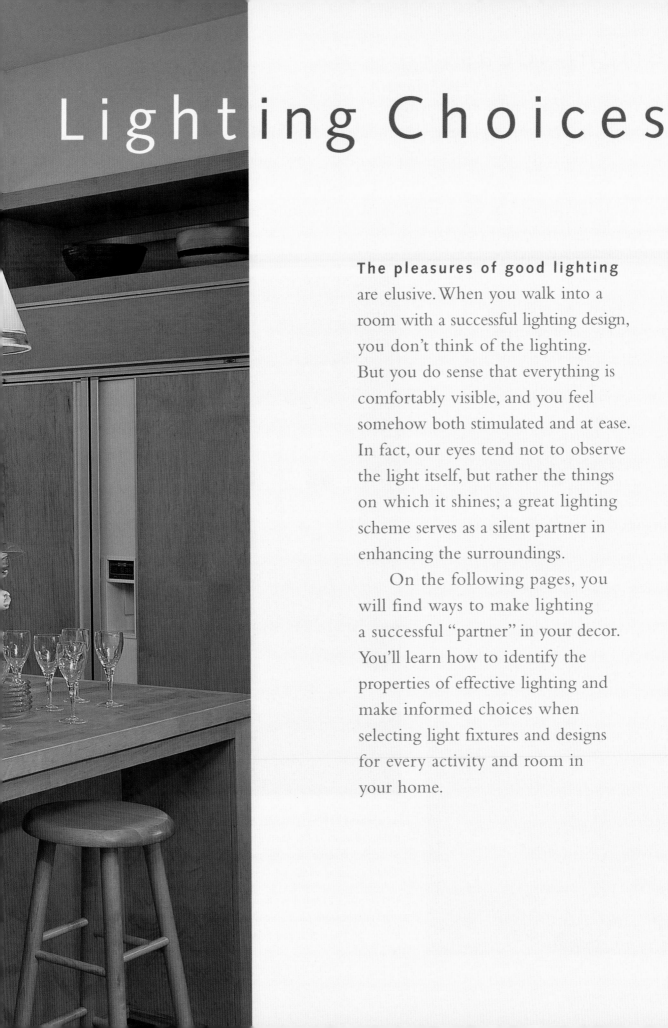

Lighting Choices

The pleasures of good lighting are elusive. When you walk into a room with a successful lighting design, you don't think of the lighting. But you do sense that everything is comfortably visible, and you feel somehow both stimulated and at ease. In fact, our eyes tend not to observe the light itself, but rather the things on which it shines; a great lighting scheme serves as a silent partner in enhancing the surroundings.

On the following pages, you will find ways to make lighting a successful "partner" in your decor. You'll learn how to identify the properties of effective lighting and make informed choices when selecting light fixtures and designs for every activity and room in your home.

Bright Ideas

Flexible, efficient, and a little bit fun—that's the plan for today's home lighting. You can choose crisp highlights or moody shadows, bold strokes or a soft, flattering wash. Or mix them together. Light sources are now more energy-efficient and fixtures are smaller. Layers of light operated by multiple controls are in. For any room in the house, you can choose lighting techniques and fixtures that will give you comfort, safety, and style.

Four Types of Lighting

Lighting has traditionally been divided into three basic categories: task, accent, and ambient. But the fourth type, decorative lighting, shouldn't be overlooked.

Task lighting is a bright light that illuminates a particular area where an activity takes place—reading, sewing, or preparing food, for example. This lighting is achieved with individual fixtures that direct a tight pattern of light onto a work surface. Task lighting must be adjustable and able to be shielded, hiding the bulb from direct sight. It's best to aim task lighting at an angle to avoid hot spots or shadows. Where possible, two light sources are better than one.

An elegant cabinet (above) highlights the collectibles within. Recessed downlights spotlight the displayed pieces, while backlighting, on a separate switch, comes from fiber optics behind the translucent back.

The lighting in this living room (left) works on a few levels: ambient light comes from built-in cove lighting, recessed downlights highlight the art on the walls, and a lamp between the sofas provides perfect task lighting.

A multilayered lighting system in a living area *consists of built-in cove lighting above the sofas, spotlights that shine on the artwork, illuminated shelving for family photographs, and an uplight on the column for soft ambient light.*

Accent lighting is used to focus attention on artwork, to highlight architectural features, to set a mood, or to provide a sense of drama. Beam spread, intensity, and color are important considerations for accent lighting. Low-voltage halogen bulbs are a good choice for this type of use.

Ambient lighting is filling a room with a soft level of general light, enough for someone to watch television by or to navigate safely through a room. An ambient glow not only makes a room more inviting, it helps people look their best, filling in harsh shadows created by stronger light. This lighting comes from indirect fixtures that provide diffuse illumination, directional fixtures aimed at a wall, or built-in lighting coves and cornices.

Decorative lighting is a fixture that draws attention to itself as an object, like the classic chandelier. Popular new options include small, decorative low-voltage pendant fixtures, neon lights, and fiber optics.

A wrought-iron chandelier *(above) provides light for the dining room table. A large mirror in the wall unit reflects light from the chandelier as well as the wonderful sunlight that comes into the room through the large windows.*

Three blown-glass pendant lights *(right), a decorative departure from the traditional chandelier, echo the three windows in this serene dining room. Recessed lights in the curved soffit highlight the painting.*

The Importance of Flexibility

Flexibility is the new byword in lighting. To achieve flexibility, you need multiple light sources or layers operated by multiple controls. Here's a look at how lighting designers approach the subject.

The art of layering. One basic rule of efficient lighting is to put light where you need it and to balance the light, creating an effective spread of dim and strong light throughout a room. The key to balancing light is layering the four different lighting types. First, identify the main activity areas or the room's focal points to direct the brightest layer of light. Next, create a middle layer to highlight interest in specific areas without detracting

from the focal points. The third layer will fill in the background. The first two layers use task or accent lighting, depending on what is being lit. The lower-level "fill" or ambient light is usually indirect. To these layers, you may add decorative fixtures.

Getting control. Dimmers and control panels can help you custom-tailor light for multiple uses and decorative effects. Dimmers—also called rheostats—enable you to control the brightness level and are energy savers. (Be aware that fluorescents can be difficult or unduly expensive to dim.) Control panels allow you to monitor a number of functions from one spot.

Beware of glare. When placing light fixtures, consider the glare they produce. Direct glare from a bare bulb is the worst kind. Remedies include deeply recessed fixtures, ones with black baffles or small apertures, clip-on louvers and shutters, silvered-bowl bulbs, and diffusing shades or covers. Reflected glare, which is light bouncing off an object into your eyes, can be avoided by placing fixtures at a 30- to 45-degree angle.

Wall sconces *cast a suffused light in this spare dining room while downlights in the rafters focus light on the table. The soft lighting creates a romantic atmosphere.*

Choosing Light Fixtures

Given the great variety of light fixtures available today, finding the right ones can be confusing and a bit complicated. Here are some points to keep in mind.

Fixture types. Basic options include movable lamps, surface-mounted ceiling and wall lights, track systems, recessed downlights, and built-in coves, cornices, valances, and soffits.

Beam pattern. One of the primary considerations is how a fixture directs light—narrow and focused or broad and diffused. For greatest efficiency, match the light distribution pattern to the lighting need.

Matching nickel-plated wall fixtures (above) are strategically placed in this bathroom to provide the most flattering light.

Leaded-glass panels (right), used as a skylight and a window, let in diffused daylight while maintaining privacy in this modern bathroom. Natural light is reflected in the large mirror over the sink while rectangular wall fixtures, only one of which is visible in the photograph, placed at the sides of the mirror provide light for grooming.

Size. Fixtures often seem smaller in the store than they will at home. Take measurements of the top choices; then hold bowls or boxes of the same sizes in place back at home to evaluate the scale. Manufacturers often produce fixtures in graded sizes, so ask about other possibilities.

Design. Personal taste will be your guide. Professionals have found that using similar fixtures throughout a home creates a sense of decorative continuity.

Cost. When calculating costs, consider the price of the fixture as well as the energy consumption and efficiency of the bulbs or tubes.

Flexibility. A lighting system should be flexible enough to accommodate changes in tastes, habits, and styles over the years. Movable lamps are flexible by design. But track systems and even recessed downlights can be changed, too.

Maintenance. For efficiency, all fixtures need to be cleaned regularly. Use easy-to-reach fixtures in kitchens, bathrooms, and work areas. For hard-to-reach areas, such as above stairs, use a fixture with a long-lived fluorescent or halogen bulb.

At either side of the sink, *stylish wall sconces are mounted directly to the seamless mirrored surface, giving the area balanced, effective light. The mirrored end walls of the built-in vanity reflect the light, effectively doubling the amount of light at the sink.*

Modern hanging pendants *(above) follow the gentle curve of the soffit and island in this kitchen while under-cabinet lights provide ample task lighting for the countertop. The lighting plays up the butter yellow walls and marble island, softening the hard-edged steel cabinets and appliances.*

Multiple light sources *(right) make this a comfortable kitchen in which to work. Two pendant lights illuminate the eating island, under-cabinet lights furnish task light for the corner countertop, and downlights in the ceiling brighten the main working area.*

Energy-Saving Options

In the average household, lighting accounts for 15 to 20 percent of all electrical power consumed. By carefully planning new lighting or making a few changes in your present habits, you can trim your energy consumption and costs. Here's a checklist of sixteen energy-saving tips to get you started:

- Switch off lights when you leave a room.
- Paint your walls light colors.
- Take advantage of daylight.
- Emphasize task lighting.
- Buy compact fluorescent bulbs.
- Dust lightbulbs regularly.
- Buy three-way bulbs.
- Use energy-saving night-lights.
- Use the lowest wattage lightbulbs possible.
- Move lamps toward the corners of rooms.
- Add dimmers to lamps and light circuits.
- Install timer switches.
- Opt for low-voltage garden lights.
- Install motion detectors and photocells outdoors.
- Make security lights fluorescent or mercury-vapor.
- Go solar to power garden lighting.

This modern kitchen *proudly demonstrates how attractive fluorescent lighting can be. Except for the trio of tiny pendants hovering near the eating countertop, all the ceiling fixtures in this room contain space-saving PL-fluorescent tubes.*

GREAT IDEAS

Living Rooms

Decorating a living room may seem more challenging than other rooms in the house. It is a public part of your home, a place where you welcome friends as well as family. You want this area to reflect something about you, your character, perhaps to showcase a special interest, and to be inviting—but one that is clearly separate from the private areas of your home. At the same time, if your living room is a place for entertaining and family use, your decorating choices should be as practical as they are beautiful.

Take a look at the photographs on the following pages. You'll find living rooms that, whether large or small, traditional or contemporary, have met this decorating challenge. Casual enough for the family to use as a gathering spot, yet elegant enough to welcome guests—these are rooms truly meant for living.

A careful arrangement of furniture *allows this room to function in multiple ways. The sofa and leather ottoman form a conversational spot near the larger window while a game table and a graphic area rug in soft neutral colors define the area in front of the fireplace.*

Antiques and traditional furniture *(left)* mix beautifully in this classic living room. The leather trunk on a stand, used as a coffee table, and the Louis XV chair with a vividly striped cushion are complemented by an array of collectibles on the mantel.

Mocha walls and silver woodwork *(below)* are a surprising color combination that creates an elegant backdrop in this living area. The architectural columns add a classic note, reiterated by the silver-blue tuxedo sofa and the silver side table.

Try **a palette of new neutrals** for an elegant look in the living room.

Make a personal statement with a family heirloom, a memento from a trip, or an antique-shop find.

No perfectly matched sets or fancy upholstery fabrics here. *Instead, it's unpretentious pieces that are comfortable and practical, a combination of family heirlooms and handsome new pieces pulled together with a low-key color palette.*

Classic rattan furniture (above), a palette of celadon and ocher, and a repeated palm motif work together to convey a sunny atmosphere redolent of lanai living. The room has a polished, pulled-together look, yet is light in spirit.

Eclectic furnishings (left) from a life of travel are set against soothing white walls and views of the garden. A vintage Tibetan prayer chest sits in front of a comfortable new sofa while a time-softened Oriental carpet underlies an old English pedestal table.

A room's **architectural elements** provide a rich backdrop for your decorating ideas.

Arches, columns, ceiling beams, and a wall of glass *(above)* are the architectural details that *provide the dramatic background for this light-filled living room.*

Elegant French windows with built-in window seats *(opposite) flank a handsome fireplace. The strong architectural elements are softened by the patterned furnishings in rich, dark colors that echo the dark marble on the fireplace.*

The Art of Display

Putting your favorite pieces on display *is like showing off a part of who you are, so you'll want the arrangement to be attractive and interesting. Shown here, clockwise from above: A modern shelving unit made up of multiple squares showcases a collection of vases and plates. A French trumeau mirror provides the backdrop for the sleek antique French horse, carved from fruitwood, on the fireplace mantel. An eclectic assortment of jugs, vases, and vintage tin atop a weathered cabinet is an artful composition unified by its soft green color. A collection of deep green pottery is casually arranged on top of an Arts-and-Crafts–style glass-fronted cabinet.*

Whether your style is country or contemporary, *there is a pleasing way to show off your favorite things. Shown here, from top to bottom: One door of a large oak armoire is purposely left open to display a colorful collection of pottery vases and bowls. Against mocha walls, an antique chest in a silvery blue color anchors a display of silver accessories—treasured family photographs in silver frames on top of the chest, an ornate mirror and sconces on the wall above, and silver-framed black-and-white photographs on the adjacent wall.*

Dining Rooms

Decorating a dining room should be simple because its requirements are straightforward. The main course is a dining-room table, and the side dishes include chairs, an overhead light fixture, and somewhere to store linens, dishes, serving pieces, and cutlery. But today's dining rooms often serve a variety of functions, including a place to do homework, pay the bills, or work on a hobby. And in many homes, dining areas are connected to another room, occupying one end of a living room or family room. So you'll want to weigh the room's functions as well as its placement in your home when making your decorating choices.

On the following pages, you will see dining rooms for quiet family suppers, places to celebrate holidays, and rooms to welcome guests. Whether formal or casual, dining rooms are an integral part of making every house a home.

A favorite porcelain pattern *(right)* inspired the graceful mural in this round dining room. Creamy white trim delineates the sage green panels while the needlepoint chair seats repeat portions of the design.

The warm atmosphere of this room *(below)* is due as much to the yellow walls and polished hardwood floors as it is to the imaginative use of salvaged architectural pieces—columns, beams, and lintel—and an urn that's now a lamp.

A beautiful painted folding screen *(opposite)* infuses this dining room with elegance and style, contributing a rich background for the fine French antique dining table flanked by assorted chairs from the 1930s and 1940s.

One-of-a-kind elements help create
a feast for the eyes.

Savor a home-cooked meal in a room
imbued with **a sense of history**.

An unexpected patchwork of brightly colored cork tiles *(above) provides a soft surface that minimizes sound in the frequently used dining room of a landmark home. The room is simply furnished with a large wood trestle table and vintage chairs.*

This dining room exudes warmth and hospitality *(opposite). A gilded chandelier, an imposing painting, and chairs and a settee pulled up to a rich wood table all give the room the look of a European country manor house, but the formality is tempered a bit by the diagonal placement of the rug.*

A **casual dining area** is a perfect
place for family and friends to gather.

A padded window seat (*opposite*) with generous pillows defines the dining area in this great room. The sturdy wood table and rattan chairs enable the space to serve as a work area between mealtimes.

White walls and bamboo shades (*left*) provide a serene backdrop for the colorful wicker chairs and cushions in this dining area. The black-and-white patterned pillows and rug play a prominent role in tying together the furnishings.

A 1950s luncheonette is the theme (*below*) in this dining area outfitted with a custom-built banquette and a restaurant table. The Fiesta ware displayed on open shelves was the inspiration for the wall colors, many of which are repeated in the bright colors of the vintage advertisements.

Kitchen Basics

The kitchen is called the heart of the home for good reason. It's where you and your family gather to cook, to eat, to socialize, and sometimes just to catch up over a quick snack or cup of coffee. In many families, the kitchen is evolving into an all-purpose room, including dining table or breakfast nook, computer desk, entertainment area, fireplace—even laundry center. It is no wonder that the kitchen is the hardest-working room in the house and probably the most complex.

Decorating the kitchen requires more planning than any other room. A successful kitchen will be well designed, efficient, and incorporate the most appropriate materials.

Peruse the photographs on the following pages for inspiration and ideas as you cook up the kitchen of your dreams.

Tiled walls add **pizzazz and practicality** to any kitchen.

A kitchen with limited wall space (above) is a great place to use strong color. The yellow-orange tile, repeated in the color of the lampshades on the chandelier, features insets of tiles depicting country scenes.

Diagonally set tiles behind the stove (opposite) in this spacious kitchen are decorated with a bouquet of flowers and fruit. A graceful vine in the same delicate colors is stenciled around the room just under the crown molding.

Creating a space for a quick meal
any time of the day
makes the kitchen more inviting.

This kitchen (above) artfully mixes many natural materials that share warm colors. The light-colored Jerusalem limestone countertop, tumbled-limestone tile backsplash, and glass pendant lights contrast with the darker cherry cabinets, oak flooring, and graceful bar stools.

A vintage round table (left) next to a window seat is just the place for a quick meal. The wood table contrasts nicely with the limestone countertops and marble and limestone floors.

A long, limestone-topped island (opposite) and ceiling-hung cabinets with glass doors on both sides define this formal kitchen. All the cabinets are crafted from lightly pickled wood and the arched door frames repeat the arch of the window over the sink.

Pale sage green cabinets and yellow walls *create a softness that's easy to live with. The cool nickel-plated fixtures and drawer pulls echo the stainless steel refrigerator. The butcher block countertops add a warm note, as do the period hanging lamps.*

A **country kitchen** is always a welcome place to be.

An assortment of red and white collectibles *(left) gives this small kitchen a perky personality. The simple white cabinets and awning-style windows provide the backdrop for canisters, vintage decorated milk glass, a farmer-boy cookie jar, and enamelware— all meant to be used as well as admired.*

An antique range *(below) was the starting point for the design of this "colonial" kitchen filled with period collectibles. The long center island has fir-topped end sections that surround a lower section equipped with a food-prep sink.*

Family Rooms

Whether you call it a great room, a family room, or a den, the family room is usually the most lived-in room in any home; its comfortable seating areas are made for relaxed conversation. Designed to be shared by family and friends, a great room often includes kitchen, dining, and living areas in one open space, so activities just flow together naturally. Sometimes a great room boasts a broad expanse of windows with great views or glass doors opening onto a deck or terrace.

Often situated off the kitchen, the family room, the great room's more modest cousin, is a relaxing spot where family members gather. A den is usually a smaller room, not necessarily near the kitchen, that is also used for family activities. By any name, the room is always the favorite in every home and deserves a warm decorating touch.

Being Together

Great rooms and family rooms are gathering spaces designed for more than one purpose: cooking and eating, socializing with family and friends, listening to music, watching television, playing games, doing homework, or just hanging out. Unifying areas where so many disparate activities take place can be a real decorating challenge, but a look at these pages reveals fresh ideas for making a family room into that one special place where your family truly lives.

A Room for All Reasons

We all have ideas about what makes up the perfect space and how we would like our family to live. As you plan your decorating scheme, keep the following considerations in mind.

Family. Look at your space and think about your family's activities. Do you like to keep an eye on the kids while cooking? Do you want to curl up on a window seat to enjoy the view? Do you need space for a desk?

Kitchen. Many great rooms and family rooms revolve around the kitchen, the place where everyone seems to end

This sun-filled family room *(left) has two seating areas: blue chenille sofas are placed on the diagonal around the fireplace, and a pair of chairs faces the window to take in the view. Both groupings rest on Persian rugs placed parallel to the walls.*

Matching red silk sofas *(above) define the gathering space in this sunny yellow great room. The red plaid chair and ottoman and the antique rug in red and gold repeat the palette; the antique coffee table and chest add a personal note.*

A sophisticated color scheme *(opposite) of black and gray against pale wood contributes to the serene and spacious look of this family room. The circular glass coffee table mirrors the glass dining table and reflects the glass cabinet doors.*

up eventually. It's the center of the home, where family gathers and where guests naturally congregate to chat with the cook. Keep this in mind as you contemplate your choice and placement of furnishings.

Lighting. Daylight through windows, skylights, or glass doors is always welcome, but the real challenge is after dark. You'll want to plan a flexible lighting scheme to divide a large room into several areas and to accommodate a range of activities from movies to quick meals.

Storage. Where family members congregate to read, play games, do homework, and listen to music, versatile storage solutions are necessary.

A gleaming copper fireplace surround (above), a beautiful wood coffee table, and a subtly designed rug lend texture and pattern in shades of copper, brown, and gold to this inviting family room.

Two sofas and a chair (right) in pale colors stand back, allowing the massive fireplace made of local stone to take command. The light-colored tile floor unifies the large room.

In this long great room *where all elements are open to view, arranging the space required thoughtful planning. A rug defines and separates the conversation area from the dining area and kitchen. The neutral color palette enhances the sun-filled space.*

Furniture Dimensions

To outfit your room, you can play around with furniture on a floor plan. One initially time-consuming but worthwhile way to do this is to cut out pieces of paper scaled to represent the size and shape of the furniture you will be using. Below are some standard dimensions for basic dining- and living-room furniture.

	Width (in inches)	Depth (in inches)
SOFA	78–90	34–38
LOVE SEAT	60–70	34–38
CHAIR	28–36	28–36
ARMLESS CHAIR	22–28	22–28
COFFEE TABLE (SQUARE)	24–48	24–48
COFFEE TABLE (RECTANGULAR)	24–48	16–28
COFFEE TABLE (ROUND)	18–32	
END TABLE	14–24	14–24
SOFA TABLE/ CONSOLE	48–72	15–20
DINING TABLE (SQUARE)	36–48	26–48
DINING TABLE (RECTANGULAR)	60–84	34–42
DINING TABLE (ROUND)	36–60	
DROP-LEAF TABLE	36–72	21–63
DINING CHAIR (WITH ARMS)	22–24	16–24
DINING CHAIR (ARMLESS)	18–22	16–24
BUFFET/LOW CABINET	48–72	16–26

Let the conversation flow
 from one room to the next
  in a gathering place
   with wide open spaces.

Natural materials *(opposite)* like the rough-edged granite countertop, pale stone floor, baskets, and dried flower garland give a relaxed feel to this great room. A casual canvas slipcover and vintage trunk used as a coffee table complete the look.

A bank of wood cabinets *(below)* echoes the gleaming hardwood floor in this serene great room. Comfortable furniture in neutral colors in the conversation area includes a rattan chair and a wood and bamboo coffee table in contrasting dark wood.

A family room that's also a media center is always a **crowd pleaser**.

A wide screen (above) set into a custom-built wall unit, complete with a projector and surround-sound equipment, makes this the ultimate in media rooms. Moviegoers can enjoy the show in the comfort of plush velvet seating.

A wall unit (right) features a compartment specially made for the television set. Comfortable chairs in a bold check and an oversized coffee table to hold books and snacks make the room family friendly.

Sofas placed at a right angle *create a cozy conversation area in front of the fireplace. When the doors of the handsome oak storage unit are opened to reveal a television set, the same seating allows an easy transition from conversation to viewing.*

By the Hearth

In front of the fireplace *is a place to relax in cozy comfort in whatever style you choose. Shown here, clockwise from above: Traditional knotty-pine paneling looks clean and contemporary around a deep charcoal-colored slate fireplace surround that's flush with the wall. A simple wood mantel, a rustic bench, and a basket to hold firewood and pinecones lend a cottage style to this hearth. A symmetrical arrangement of white ironstone pieces and topiary reinforces the classic style of this painted-wood fireplace mantel.*

Rustic or sophisticated, *a fireplace adds warmth and a feeling of hospitality to any room. Shown here, clockwise from left: A fireplace made of picturesque, uneven clinker bricks is the perfect spot to display vintage treasures that complement the collection of paintings on the wall above. A flush-mounted fireplace and niche for wood are lined with hand-painted tiles that pick up the soft blue of the stained wall. A family-room fireplace just off the kitchen is dramatically framed by colorful, custom relief tiles and quieter hearth tiles.*

Home Offices

Creating a work space at
home is an exciting idea. In most
homes, however, finding room for
a home office might present a few
challenges. But potential office space
is almost always hiding, so to speak,
in plain sight. Identifying it simply
requires a shift in perspective.
Perhaps you are fortunate enough
to have a spare room. But the
most common way to squeeze in
a home office is to borrow space,
diplomatically, from an existing
room so as not to disturb the room's
original purpose. Or if the option
is available to spread out more, you
could take over space in an attic,
basement, or garage.

On the following pages, you
will see some home offices that are
grand and some that were carved
from small spaces, some that look
more like offices and others that
look more like home. You'll be sure
to find lots of ideas here that can be
adapted to your space and budget.

Creative Home Work

Bringing your work space home is a wonderful concept, but it raises some practical questions. Which room in the house will be the best place? What, really, do you need in the way of equipment and furniture? What's the best way to set things up, taking into account your personal work style as well as the nature of your work? And, while you're answering these questions, don't forget to add the touches that can make the space a comfortable and attractive part of your home.

Gearing Up

Some experts have said there are only two essentials for a functional home office: a comfortable chair and a door that closes. To make an office that really works for you, though, there are probably a few more.

Start with your work surface. Do you need a desk or another type of work surface? What shape does it need to be and what type of surface do you prefer to work on—wood, plastic, laminate? Be sure to choose a chair with an adjustable seat and armrests to protect your spine. Studies show that good equipment properly aligned helps reduce aches and injuries.

Make a list and measure all the electronic equipment you'll need to see where it will fit best. And make sure you allow for proper lighting. Natural light is great, but you'll need ambient and task lighting too. Be aware of glare, especially when finding a place for your computer screen.

A door that closes may preserve the peace as well as your privacy, but it isn't always possible. You can establish a sense of privacy by the way you orient your work surface or by using a screen or file cabinets to mark off the space.

A Japanese-inspired home office *has a rug that resembles overlapping tatami mats and Shoji-screen–like sliding doors. The cleanly styled space has glass doors that open onto a deck, a place to take a break from work and enjoy the view.*

A built-in wall unit *(left)* provides ample storage space and a Parsons-type table serves as a desk in this tidy home office. Tailored window treatments in white let in plenty of natural light. With the simple decor and muted color scheme, the room is ready for serious work.

A custom-built desk *(below)* fits the angles of a large bay window and fills the space that was once a dining area off the kitchen. The desk has a rugged cast-concrete surface and baskets that slide in and out of cubbies for storage.

A modern house with soaring ceilings (above) allows for a balcony that is large enough to accommodate a home office for both homeowners as well as a media room for the family.

An architect's home work space (opposite) is a handsomely appointed room with a wall of framed black-and-white photographs of technological wonders and lots of natural light.

Getting Organized

Although the electronic revolution has promised a paper-free office, it has yet to materialize. To plan your storage scheme as efficiently as possible, make a list of everything you will need from pencils and paper clips to research materials and file folders. Next, decide where each item will go, dividing the items on the list into the following four groups: things you use daily, weekly, occasionally, and rarely.

Plan to place whatever you use daily within arm's reach on the desktop or in a nearby drawer or shelf. Store materials used weekly elsewhere in the office, but in an accessible place. Things you use occasionally can go anywhere that's out of your way. For the last group, be especially ruthless. Try to recycle or toss out things in this group that you do not use. It will free up space for what you need on a daily basis.

Home offices can be found in almost any room of the house but often work best in the most **unexpected places**.

An ingenious use of forgotten space, *this tiny home office under the stairway has everything an office requires: a desk with storage space, a comfortable chair, adequate lighting, and even a favorite picture on the wall.*

Finding space for a home office *(left) can be as simple as looking up. At least it was for a family who turned the attic of their 1913 home into an office for two. The walls and ceiling fitted with fir are original.*

A landing on the second floor *(below) is large enough for a shelf-lined home office that is open to the gathering space below. The standard hog-wire fencing used for the railings and the straightforward office furniture create a clean, contemporary look.*

Find a space for your desk, add some shelves, and you have the formula for **a cozy office**.

With an emphasis on comfort and feminine charm (above), this home office has a pine desk set into a beadboard recess and an upholstered easy chair. Built-in shelving offers storage and display space.

In one corner of a kitchen (opposite), the cabinets and countertop were extended to create a desk and storage space with a corkboard for important notes. An upholstered chair adds comfort and color.

All it takes is **one great wall** and
an Internet connection to create an
efficient home office.

Handsome rosewood built-ins *(opposite)* constructed to fit the angle of the soaring ceiling provide lots of storage space for this home office. The desk alcove has room to display framed diplomas.

White file cabinets topped with a long granite surface *(below)* makes a desk for two with open and glass-doored shelves above. Oak office chairs and lime green walls add a warm note.

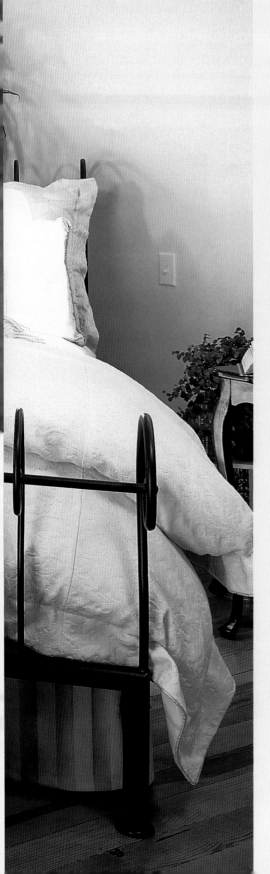

Dreamy Bedrooms

Bedrooms are restful retreats and, as life becomes busier, having a place to renew energy becomes even more important. By their private nature, bedrooms are a true reflection of your personal style. If you are designing your own bedroom, you only have to please you. It can be bright with florals, cozy and romantic, or sleek and simple. The bedroom can be uniquely yours in a way that no other room in the house can be. If you are setting up a guest bedroom, it should be welcoming, but not so full of personality that it overwhelms; and if it will double as a study, be sure to plan for both uses.

So think about what makes you happy and what speaks to your interests. That knowledge is all you need to create the bedroom of your dreams, along with some inspiration from the great ideas found on the following pages.

A parquet floor *(above) has a wide rectangle of darker wood that repeats the angular headboard and contrasts with the rounded legs of the night table. A sophisticated putty color ties everything together.*

A decidedly eclectic room *(opposite) is pulled together with a pale peach and white color scheme: sponge-painted walls with a graceful stenciled border under the crown molding and a pickled floor with a diamond design.*

A Bigger Space

A master bedroom suite, including bathroom and dressing area, is large enough for many uses. Of course, you sleep there, but you can also read, lounge, exercise, work, and pamper yourself. Your bedroom can be a self-contained space full of amenities, which may become your favorite place to hang out.

When decorating a master bedroom suite, you want to think about how the rooms flow into one another. Delineate the rooms with their own distinctive touches, but consider using a similar color in all the areas to help tie them together and give the entire space a harmonious look.

Even in a room where many activities take place, think about carefully editing your furniture and accessories so that the area seems more spacious. The goal of a decorating plan for a suite of rooms is to have balance: in color, in style, and in furnishings.

A love of French antiques defines the decor in this bedroom. *The painted cane bedstead is graced with a lovely French quilt and the vintage sky-blue nightstand is French, too. The French antique bedside lamps are actually music boxes, operated by turning a crank on their backs.*

A traditional quilt *(left)* in soft autumn gold, green, and rust was the starting point for the color scheme in this restful bedroom. The bed, with a curved headboard silhouetted against pale gold walls, sports a profusion of pillows in the same colors.

Blue is a restful color *(below)* often chosen for bedrooms, and here it's mixed with the cream color of the four-poster bed and nightstand. Two different blue and cream checked fabrics are used as companions to a traditional floral coverlet.

An imaginative combination of fabrics creates **a comfortable place to rest**.

A **red plaid blanket** (right) and red pillows add a warm touch to this predominately green and yellow bedroom. The salvaged shutters and old icebox used as a nightstand give the room the look of a vacation cottage.

Red, a vibrant color (below) not often thought of as restful, is used to create a sophisticated bedroom with a maple sleigh bed and oversized ottoman. The mix of patterns works nicely against the solid-color walls and the ice-blue sofa adds a cool contrast to the warm palette.

The power of red works wonders
in any bedroom.

Against light yellow walls, a red and green color scheme *is carried out in camp blankets from the 1920s, 1930s, and 1940s. The striped fabric on the bed is new but blends right in. Beadboard paneling on the walls lends a cottage feel, while eclectic vintage pieces—including an old camp sign—add fun.*

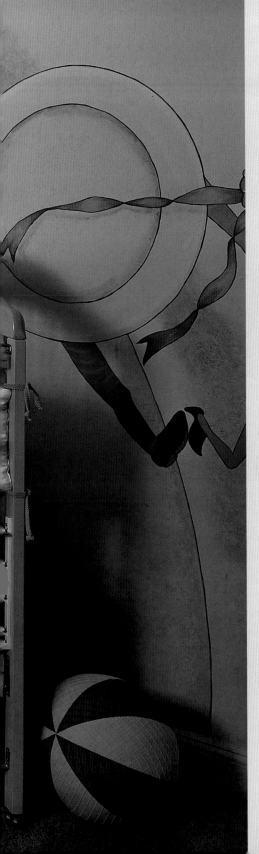

Children's Rooms

Go to your room! What a pleasant banishment if the room is as inviting and wonderful to be in as the ones shown here. A bedroom for a child is more than a room for sleeping. It is also a place to do schoolwork, listen to music, play games, sprawl on the floor, roughhouse, read, build models, daydream, visit with friends, and keep innumerable possessions. That's asking a lot, so you'll need to plan carefully to create a room that serves all those functions, yet is comfortable and inviting—and has enough staying power to require only minimal redecorating every few years.

The ultimate experts on what kids like best are kids themselves. So make your children partners in the planning process, looking at pleasing color combinations, creative ways with paint or fabric, and interesting uses of furniture. Together you can create a room they will enjoy.

For Kids Only

Where do you start? You can start by focusing on the kids. These days kids are more style conscious than ever, about everything from running shoes to bed linens. They want their rooms to look cool. That means getting the right colors, the right furniture, and the right accessories—ones that are not trendy and will grow with your child. Even if your child isn't old enough yet to have strong opinions about decor, it's only a matter of time before individual preferences kick in. So you'll want a room that both meets your needs and pleases your child.

Who's in Charge?

A nicely decorated room may look great to parents, but its style and contents must be geared to the child for it to be truly enjoyed. Consider the following:

Age. Obviously, the furniture and accessories should be appropriate for your child's age, but they should also be adaptable to their changing needs.

Personality. Include children's interests, and ask for their opinion, as you create a decorating scheme.

Activities. Make sure you plan for the many activities that will take place in the room.

A four-poster bed (above) covered with a perky red plaid duvet is a great place for kids and their furry friends to hang out. Simple decor with classic furniture is ageless and adapts easily to changing tastes as children grow.

This under-the-eaves bedroom (left) has trompe l'oeil windows to open up the space and a profusion of colorful fabrics to make it inviting. The maple dresser has a darker-stained top to coordinate with the cherry sleigh bed.

A collection of folk art pieces, *including toys, birdhouses, a weather vane, and a jaunty block quilt on the bed, makes this a perfect bedroom for a budding collector.*

Scale. Children should have a sense of control over their environment. They should be able to hang up clothes, reach toys and books, and sit in chairs their size.

Color. Young children need visual stimulation, and most kids love bright colors. But consider your child's taste and incorporate a favorite color into the room somewhere.

Maintenance. The younger the child, the more durable and easy to clean the materials should be. For kids of any age, make the room easy to maintain no matter who is in charge of tidying up.

Safety. Whatever the design, a safe environment is critical. Review the literature on all surfaces and products, and stay up-to-date on product recalls before you make major purchases.

Classic toile curtains and an antique French chandelier *evoke a Paris hotel room for a new baby whose crib becomes a throne when enrobed in sheer linen curtains. A Manet print in an elegant frame hung from upholstery cord adds the finishing touch.*

A room is born—and just in time **to welcome the new baby**.

An antique sideboard *(left) becomes a changing table that holds baby's supplies in a room with a sophisticated violet and gold color scheme. A simple wall-mounted wooden shelf with pegs adds storage and display space.*

In a sunny yellow room *(below), a garden is painted on the walls and the window treatments evoke blue skies with white clouds. Bright pink and white plaid crib linens are topped with a floral quilt.*

The rewards of sharing a bedroom are special secrets and comfort in the dark—think of it as **a sleepover every night**.

Four-poster twin beds with matching star quilts *folded over chenille bedspreads outfit a dream bedroom for two sisters. The muted color scheme and classic furnishings are easily adaptable as they grow.*

Wallpaper with pairs of cherries (left) establishes the theme in this bedroom for twins. A bracket shelf placed just under the crown molding displays their two-of-each toy collection. The mismatched cribs sport coordinated but not matching linens.

An older sibling and baby share this room (below). The striped wallpaper has a traditional look but is topped with a water-color border design of animals. The large braided chenille rug softens the old fir floor.

Rub-a-dub-dub! *Nursery-rhyme characters enliven the wall of this child's room and supply the color scheme for the various blue and yellow fabrics used to decorate the room. Star and moon drawer knobs carry out the theme.*

A collection of birdhouses *(left)* provided the inspiration for this imaginative room. A talented muralist created a tree: the branches are hand painted; the leaves are stamped. Several of the birdhouses hang from the ceiling on fishing line.

An under-the-sea theme *(below)* started with sponge-painted sea green walls that match the colors in the area rug. The one-of-a-kind frog toy chest feels right at home with the other sea creatures.

Rooms that **tell a tale** appeal to the child in all of us.

A Place to Play

Since play is child's work, *it's important to have a space devoted to that pursuit. Shown here, clockwise from above: A maple schoolroom table from the 1950s is just the right size for children to gather, and behind it an old valet rack holds toys and vintage finds. A child's study area is designed for work and play with spaces for books, toys, a computer, and a corkboard display. One end of a family room becomes a playroom with a cleverly designed room divider that is play space and storage space in one. A built-in bookcase is an ideal place for toy and book storage, especially with an upholstered child-size chair and ottoman nearby.*

Play spaces that re-create *a child's favorite place are imaginative and fun. Shown here, from top to bottom: A dormer window in an under-the-eaves bedroom is the perfect place for a "tree house" complete with trompe l'oeil windows as well as a real one. "All aboard" in this room means climb into the bed that's designed to look like a train engine or play in the window-seat caboose that holds toys and books in open display shelves and cabinets.*

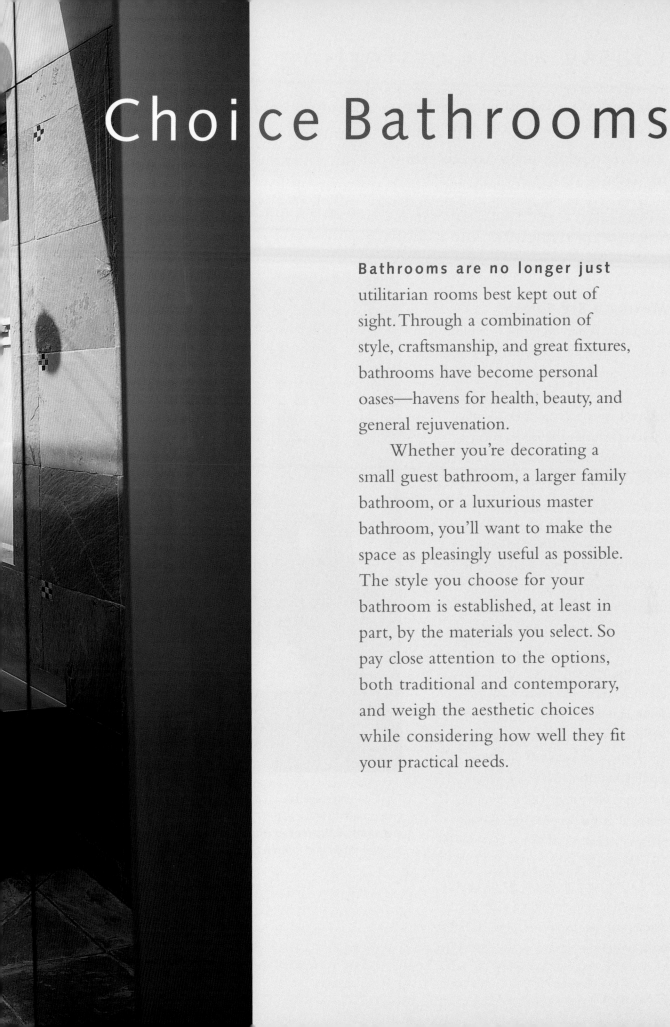

Choice Bathrooms

Bathrooms are no longer just utilitarian rooms best kept out of sight. Through a combination of style, craftsmanship, and great fixtures, bathrooms have become personal oases—havens for health, beauty, and general rejuvenation.

Whether you're decorating a small guest bathroom, a larger family bathroom, or a luxurious master bathroom, you'll want to make the space as pleasingly useful as possible. The style you choose for your bathroom is established, at least in part, by the materials you select. So pay close attention to the options, both traditional and contemporary, and weigh the aesthetic choices while considering how well they fit your practical needs.

Classy and Comforting

The bathroom is no longer the most standardized room in the house. It has developed its own personality. Basic or elegant, modern or traditional, it should be warm enough to invite you to primp but simple enough to get you out quickly. To make your bathroom as individual as you are, it helps to have both information and inspiration. When a bathroom looks good and functions well, you can be sure that great planning went into its realization.

Making a Big Splash

To create a bathroom that is beautiful, bold, and especially comfortable, you'll want to consider its many components.

Surfaces are a major element in a bathroom's style. There are now more choices for materials than ever, and a freer mixing of these materials. You can choose stone, tile, wood, laminate, vinyl, or concrete for walls, floors, and sink and tub surrounds.

There is also a larger selection of fixtures and fittings. Sinks can be pedestal or wall-hung. Tubs can be freestanding models, encased in a surround, or part of a tub/shower unit. Toilets come in new styles, new colors, and with new efficiency: low-flush toilets are now mandated in many communities as a result of a growing attention to water conservation.

There is an emphasis on better lighting in bathrooms, too, for both grooming and safety. Think about the universal or barrier-free bath for the physically challenged and as your family ages (see page 243).

Larger bathrooms can be divided for multiple uses, including exercise equipment, saunas, steam showers, and walk-in dressing areas.

Tumbled-limestone tile *on the walls and floor of this small bathroom give it warmth and a natural texture. The decor is simple with a mahogany vanity topped with a large mirror and a striped sheer window shade that diffuses the light.*

A greenhouse window (left) adds daylight, views, and display space in this small bathroom; its translucent panels assure privacy. The pale stone, light-colored wood, and glass shower doors expand the sense of space.

A comfortably large bathroom (below) takes advantage of the wonderful light that comes through the window. A long mirror-faced cabinet has flush-mounted vertical incandescent tubes for grooming and under-the-cabinet light to illuminate the counter. The open fir vanity with a hand-tooled marble top accommodates two people.

A large, sunny bathroom *(above)* in an
Arts-and-Crafts–style home has a classic
freestanding tub, twin pedestal sinks,
frame-and-panel wainscoting, period-
style wall sconces, and rich marble floor
tiles. Flat lace curtains filter the light.

Subtly colored walls *(right)* and gilt
stenciling around the archway set the
tone for this bathroom that mixes new
and old. The pedestal sink is new but in
a classic style, while the wall cabinet, the
architectural detail next to the arch, and
the chair in the alcove are all antiques.

Classic fixtures and period wall treatments
with a personal touch or two
add **cozy comfort** to any bathroom.

This double sink has the look of an antique country table *with its turned wooden legs and limestone top, and the fir-framed, mirrored medicine cabinet is large enough for two. Tiled wainscoting, a sisal rug, and tulip-shaped wall sconces add to the style.*

A universally designed or **barrier-free bathroom** is accessible to everyone regardless of age or ability to move around.

Universal Design

All of us are young once, most of us grow old, and any of us can become disabled at any time. A bathroom design that considers the needs of all people who will use it—children, the elderly, and handicapped people—is called a universal, or barrier-free, design.

The National Kitchen and Bath Association (NKBA) and the Americans with Disabilities Act (ADA) of 1990 have set standards for the placement of fixtures. They recommend a clear floor space at least 30 by 48 inches in front of each fixture, although the spaces for individual fixtures may overlap. Below are their recommendations for clearances along with additional guidelines.

Guidelines and clearances

- A room at least 8 by 8 feet.
- Doorways at least 36 inches wide, with the doors opening out.
- A center space of 60 by 60 inches for a turnaround.
- Showers at least 42 inches square or 60 inches long to accommodate a wheelchair.
- Toilet and shower seats 17 to 19 inches high.
- A sink 34 inches above the floor with 27-inch knee space.
- Light switches and electrical outlets no higher than 42 inches above the floor.
- Use of grab bars, paddle-style faucet handles, and antiscald devices on the faucets.
- Use of laminated or tempered glass, or specially approved plastic.
- Use of slip-resistant flooring.

A marble-lined shower *(above)* *with an adjustable shower head and grab bars, a large padded bench, and a padded curb looks elegant and is easy to use.*

A barrier-free pedestal sink *(opposite), an angled mirror, and a cantilevered counter make this an accessible bathroom. The tub's grab bars and sinkside shower controls are attractive and the padded tub seat adds a colorful note.*

Bonus Spaces

While most living spaces are meant to be social places, there is no denying that most of us yearn for a spot that offers comfortable solitude. Sometimes such nooks and crannies are part of a home's architecture— even an alcove, for example, can provide a place of refuge. But sometimes you have to create them yourself, and a sheltered, private area is well worth the effort. Part of the fun is designing a space that appears as inviting from without as it is comfortable from within.

You may have a spare room waiting for just such a purpose, an unused corner newly discovered, or a space you can rethink. Whether your bonus space is as simple as a comfortable chair tucked between book-lined walls or as complex as a built-in window seat with storage below, it always enriches your home.

Cozy Retreats

For a bit of respite, nothing could be easier than placing an overstuffed chair and a lamp in a corner. But there are many opportunities to create a sheltered spot where there isn't one already. Think about the possibilities in your home: the end of a hallway, a large stair landing, one end of a long living room, the corner in an L-shaped bedroom, an enclosed porch, or under the eaves in the attic are just a few of the choices.

Wish Fulfillment

What makes you happy? To create a satisfying nook, you'll want to think about the ways you relax. You may want a seat by the window to enjoy the view and to daydream. You may need a small desk, the perfect spot for journal keeping or letter writing. You may want a chaise longue to read a good novel or catch a quick nap. Perhaps you'll need a place to work on your favorite hobby.

A small alcove next to a closet *(left) is just the spot for delicate furnishings like a sheer-silk–slipcovered armchair and a dressing table that doubles as a writing desk.*

Elegance in an attic hideaway *(above) starts with a chaise longue placed at an angle to help camouflage the narrow width of the room. Sheer linen panels on the window with pale-colored bands on the leading edges let in the light.*

A hallway that ends abruptly *(opposite) is transformed into a comfortable spot by a mural that resembles a wall in an Italian villa, an Italian chest of drawers, and a bronze-figure lamp. A simple window treatment in the same colors as the mural completes the space.*

How will you furnish this extra space? You might want a comfortable chair or a cushion-tossed daybed that will do double duty as a guest bed. Perhaps your space calls for a built-in seat with storage underneath. And you'll always need good lighting, whether you are near a window or not.

What are the finishing touches? Make this space reflect your special interests. Perhaps you'll want only a vase of flowers to display your skills in the garden. Or a chessboard set up ready for play. Perhaps your nook is a place to showcase a prized collection or a place to keep the books you're eager to read.

A cozy but functional mudroom *(above) was created with a built-in bench and cabinets. Beadboard, sprightly fabrics, and a red slate floor give the space its charm.*

A built-in daybed with toy storage underneath *(opposite, top) in an enclosed porch off the kitchen makes great use of what could have been wasted space. It's now used as a play area, a sunroom, and a place for sleepovers.*

An unused corner, **extra space just waiting to be found**, is transformed by built-ins.

A small room (below) becomes more functional with built-in cabinets that house enclosed storage and bookshelves. Sitting atop the storage is a twin-size mattress that's a sofa by day and a guest bed at night.

A Seat with a View

It's difficult to imagine a cozier spot *than a seat by the window. Shown here, clockwise from above: In a child's bedroom, a window seat has storage below, while cheerful fabrics and wide-striped walls add to the charm. A captain's bed and bookshelves built into a wide hallway provide a comfortable seat for reading, an extra bed for guests, and storage, too. A bay window between the kitchen and the dining area is the perfect place for a pillow-covered seat to enjoy the view or to watch the cook.*

Window-seat styles vary to suit the room. Shown here, clockwise from left: A custom-built wall unit with a seat is situated opposite the window in this room for a better angle on the view. A window seat in a long bay window in a living room becomes a cozy gathering space with the addition of a round table and two occasional chairs. A contemporary window seat with a perky striped cloud shade is tucked between two bookcases in a child's bedroom.

Cheery Sunrooms

Basking in warmth and light is one of life's great pleasures. So the sunroom is often a favorite place for people to gather. It's a unique space with a style most often inspired by the life of a garden and expressed in a love of sunlight and a view of the outdoors. A sunroom can be part of any room in the house—the living room, dining room, or kitchen—or it can be a room of its own. Whether large or small, a place to entertain friends or a space for quiet contemplation, a sunroom has an air of unassuming informality.

As you leaf through these pages, you will see how many fresh and delightful ways the sunroom can be interpreted, from dramatic rooms with sweeping views to simple rooms that overlook the back garden. Outfitted with your favorite things, a sunroom offers a place to relax comfortably at home.

Framing the View

A sunroom is the perfect place to enjoy what nature has to offer, no matter what the weather or the season. It can be a room for gardening, a relaxing retreat, a space for dining, or a peaceful home office. Whatever the purpose, you'll need furniture appropriate to its use—a wooden table for dining, a comfortable office chair, or a rustic potting table. By blending your own indoor and outdoor furnishings, accessories, and plants, you can create a truly inviting room and one that always lets the sun shine in.

An enclosed porch serves as a family room *with plenty of seating for family and friends and a dining table that is also used for games. The large windows with views of the garden are the focal point, so the decor is subdued.*

This garden room uses natural materials—limestone flooring, bamboo furniture, and a table base made from a tree trunk—as a link to the garden outside. The gauzy linen panels filter the light but do not obscure the view.

The Inside Story

Naturally, sunrooms are rooms that have plenty of natural light streaming in, but they have other elements in common as well. Sunrooms often have a relaxed approach to furnishing and a decor that expresses a warm sense of hospitality. There is an emphasis on easy comfort. Seating should be flexible, allowing you to pull up a chair for a guest or to gather around a game table.

Choose furniture made of wood, wicker, or metal wirework. Include a small table for casual dining, plus side tables to hold books or drinking glasses. You'll want to add accents that reflect your personal style and plenty of lush green plants.

Although light floods in during the day, you'll want to have appropriate lighting near seating areas for reading or other close tasks at other times. And be sure to combine ambient lighting with reading lamps for nighttime. On the practical side, curtains and shades can filter out hot afternoon sun, and an overhead fan can supply cool breezes.

Getting away from it all is so easy
in a room flooded with sunlight.

A bevy of pillows in a variety of floral fabrics *sets the mood in this sunny garden room. The blue wicker furniture is the perfect foil for the print fabrics; the delicate wire table holds a floral tea set and decorative floral hatboxes, and a flowered rug underscores it all.*

A wooden column (left) salvaged from an antebellum home in Georgia graces the opening to this cozy sunroom. Simple furnishings allow the eye to focus on the view of trees and sky.

An enclosed porch (below), furnished with wicker furniture, bamboo shades, and cupboards made of antique boards, has an appropriately outdoorsy color scheme of sky blue and grass green.

A custom-designed greenhouse addition (above) opens up the adjacent kitchen and provides an airy garden room furnished with wicker pieces for dining.

Flowering plants and trees abound (opposite) in this lush greenhouse addition. The flagstone floor, floral curtains, and antique rattan furniture add to the ambience.

Garden rooms capture the elusive
pleasures of nature.

Porches & Patios

In the quest for more living space, there's one spot that shouldn't be overlooked: the rooms just outside the door. What better way to enlarge your space and enjoy dramatic views than to expand into the outdoor landscape?

Your outdoor space may be classic and formal or fluid and naturalistic. You may be yearning for an inviting entertainment space, a quiet private refuge, or simply a spot for sunbathing and stargazing. Or maybe you want it all. You don't have to settle for a boring patio slab or an uninviting back porch. Interior design ideas have migrated outdoors. New shapes, textures, colors, and amenities abound. Take a look at the ideas on the following pages to extend your living space.

Open-Air Elegance

As fun as it is to daydream about a new outdoor living space, careful planning is what will make the dream a reality. First, you'll want to define the outdoor areas: determine what activities will take place where, think about which family members will use the area, and decide whether you want a formal or informal outdoor environment. The style you choose and the materials you utilize—brick, stone, wood—should be compatible with the architecture of your house and appropriate to your climate.

Good Living Outdoors

A patio or porch should be useful and comfortable as well as visually complementary to its surroundings. As you plan your outdoor living space, think about the following issues.

Meeting your needs. Your design should be able to accommodate your family's favorite activities, from relaxation and casual gatherings to children's games, barbecues, and entertaining.

Protecting privacy. As an extension of your indoor living space, your porch or patio should offer the same feeling of privacy as interior rooms do.

On this classic front porch *(above), the painted floor provides a soft background for the cheery colors of the wood chairs—all flea-market finds. The chair colors are a new take on a primary color scheme.*

At one end of a long porch *(left), windows partially enclose the space to create a protected outdoor sitting area. A color scheme of dark red brick and forest green furniture is lightened up with floral and gingham fabrics.*

This wide porch is a welcoming place to entertain. *The painted dark gray floor complements the weathered shingles, and the white wicker furniture with cheerful vintage-print pillows picks up the crisp white trim.*

Being aware of safety. Choose materials that will not become slippery when wet and that are not sharp or uneven for children's games. Keep passageways from house to porch or patio safe and unobstructed. Provide adequate lighting on the porch or patio and along any outdoor path leading to it.

Using color well. As in a beautiful indoor room, colors should have a relationship to one another. Think about colors that will complement the exterior of your home and that harmonize with the earth tones of the landscape around it.

Thinking about the transition. A patio or porch should entice people outdoors. So be sure to consider the transition from the inside of your house to the outside.

White latticework panels *(right)* transform a simple deck into an outdoor living room, giving it privacy and protection from the sun. The brightly striped curtains, handsome pillows, and cushions on the wicker furniture were made from specially treated outdoor fabrics.

A small front porch *(below)* becomes an outdoor foyer with the addition of a floor of glazed Arts-and-Crafts–style tiles in an array of beautiful colors. A modest wood bench provides a place to sit.

Little can compare to the pleasure of **sitting on a porch** on a lazy afternoon.

Simple canvas curtains *furnish privacy for this front porch, making it a great place for family activities. The cocoa-colored wicker furniture and printed rug coordinate nicely with the stucco on the house's exterior.*

Dining Alfresco

When the weather is great, *dining outdoors is delectable. Clockwise from above: In one part of a courtyard, a round table with upholstered chairs, set beneath a collection of hand-painted Italian plates, welcomes diners. A stone-pillared pavilion with a built-in barbecue and hearth is the perfect setting for dining outdoors. Tucked into an intimate courtyard and covered with an open arbor, this outdoor dining room is a gracious setting for entertaining.*

Backyard decks offer wonderful spaces *for outdoor dining. Shown at left, a low deck ringed with tall plants provides a private space to dine or just relax; the passage from the house to the deck has Saltillo tile flooring, an arbor roof, and a trickling fountain. And below, a handsome, dark-stained cedar deck with a skirt that matches the house's siding has plenty of seating for family and friends, with built-in benches as well as a dining table and chairs.*

Storage Solutions

There's no question that where people come together, things accumulate. And to have a handle on those things, to create efficient, usable storage for all of them, will make your home a more beautiful place.

As you'll see on the following pages, storage can be as attractive as it is functional. Storage solutions can be unobtrusive or open to view, minimal or elaborate, depending on your needs. Some of the storage ideas shown here may be basic and some more imaginative, but all of them offer great ideas for creating ways to store things in every room of the house. As you explore the options in your house, maybe you'll find storage space you never knew you had. Adequate storage space is essential to making life easier around the house.

Everything in Its Place

It can be a daunting task to find places for everything when there is just more stuff than there is closet space. One way to approach your storage needs is to identify your needs, categorize the items, and then come up with solutions. So first, think about everything you need to store. Next, categorize the items—clothes, collectibles, sports equipment, books, toys—and decide which room is the most appropriate place for storing each group. Then consider the great variety of storage containers and make sure you choose ones that are large enough to meet your needs.

Attractive and Useful

Storage solutions can be as simple as shelves, wall hooks, and boxes, or as elaborate as custom-built wall units.

Hidden storage. In addition to the usual closets and pantry, think about under-the-bed storage, as well as under the eaves if you have attic space.

Display storage. Books open to view are a given, but you can display your collectibles, your grandmother's china, and other keepsakes in a china cabinet or on open shelves.

Built-in storage. A custom-made wall unit tailored to your needs is a great solution. But also consider a window seat with storage underneath.

Freestanding storage. Choose an armoire or sideboard in a style that works with the rest of your furnishings. But also think about smaller pieces like file cabinets in the family room or a rolling cart in the kitchen.

Dual-purpose storage. A trunk used as a coffee table or a wicker basket with a cover used as a nightstand provide storage beyond their primary purpose. Also consider decorative tins to store sewing supplies or a collection of baskets to store office supplies.

An old wicker trunk (above), providing storage as well as a surface to display collectible books and a vintage watering can, creates an attractive assemblage in a corner next to a new wooden cupboard painted and distressed for a vintage look.

Custom-built shelves (opposite) follow the curve of the window wall in this living room and fill the space around the slate-faced fireplace. The built-in storage has ample room for books as well as display space for favorite objects.

Open or closed, dining-room storage helps
make entertaining easier.

A beautiful garlanded hutch (above) is the focal point in this dining area next to the kitchen. The hutch has display space on top, a plate rack in the middle, and small square drawers and cabinets below.

Open shelves are a must (left) in this diminutive dining area because there is no room for another piece of furniture, especially a cabinet with doors that open and close. The solution is an attractive display of china and glassware that is easily accessible.

A warm wood sideboard (opposite) was built into a wide arch between the dining room and the entry hall. The handsome piece provides ample storage and doubles as a serving area for buffet dinners.

Multipurpose, flexible shelves are
the perfect ingredients for kitchen storage.

What cook doesn't yearn for more storage space? *In this rustic country kitchen, that space was found on the sink wall above the tiled backsplash, where long shelves with sturdy brackets hold everyday dishes as well as provide display space for favorite flea-market serving trays.*

A long butcher-block–topped island (above) has storage for pots and pans on the kitchen side and, on the dining-room side, shelves for cookbooks and a display of favorite pottery. These shelves repeat the look of the shelves on the back wall of the kitchen.

This kitchen (left) combines sunlight and storage. The cabinet wall consists of glass shelves sandwiched between two translucent vertical layers: frosted, rimless glass door panels in the front and a wall of translucent panels along the exterior of the house.

Organization is important *(right) with a new baby, but with triplets it is paramount. A custom-built wall unit provides drawers for clothes, space for diaper changes, and storage for diaper bins and laundry hampers, as well as open shelves for displaying favorite toys.*

A large dressing area *(above) was created at one end of a bedroom, along the wall leading to the bathroom, by building floor-to-ceiling closets, which are reflected in the mirror of the wall unit. The teak units provide ample storage space as well as a place for grooming.*

White laminate built-in cabinets *(left) provide lots of storage space along one wall of a bedroom, and the mirrors above it stretch the space. The flush-front doors and drawers lend a modern, European look that works well in a simply styled bedroom.*

Ample storage space is at the top of everyone's wish list.

A spectacular view (above) defines this upper-floor bedroom and built-in furnishings keep the room's decor simple and clean. A captain's-style bed with two rows of drawers eliminates the need for a chest of drawers and elevates the bed to take advantage of the view.

A built-in unit (left) in this bedroom, extending from the bathroom door to the closet door, serves as a headboard, a bookshelf, and a place for display. The simply styled teak unit becomes a dramatic focal point for the room.

You know you're
home again in
a room filled with
personal favorites.

Books *(right) are often among the most beloved of personal collections, and this white built-in bookcase topped with crown molding gives them their due.*

Bigger is not necessarily better *(above). Here thick boards are supported by two A-frame structures to create a unique display for family photographs around the television.*

Size Matters

Knowing the size and shape of books and media accessories ensures that these items fit the allotted space. So take inventory of what you own and then measure them before buying or building a storage unit.

Standard sizes of books

ART BOOK 15 by 11 inches

TEXTBOOK 11 by 9 inches

STANDARD BOOK 9½ by 7 inches

PAPERBACK 6⅞ by 4¼ inches

Standard sizes of media accessories

DVD 7½ by 5⅜ inches

LP OR LASER DISC 12⅜ by 12⅜ inches

VIDEOTAPE 7½ by 4⅛ inches

CD 5 by 5⅝ inches

AUDIOCASSETTE 4¼ by 2¾ inches

A family room (above) becomes a home library with built-in floor-to-ceiling shelves constructed around the French doors that lead to the patio. The bright red doors and the Saltillo tile floor give an unexpectedly casual feel to this room.

A storage unit (right) that was built into one wall of a family room contains a closet surrounded by cubbyholes used to hold books and display favorite pieces. Light fixtures installed high on the wall spotlight the collectibles.

Built to Fit

Some of the most useful storage is the kind *built to exact specifications. Shown here, clockwise from above: An extra wide window seat in the family room has open shelves under the seat for storing serving dishes reserved for special occasions. A built-in seat contains large file drawers that keep important papers close at hand but out of sight. For a busy family, a shoe storage closet near the front door is a clever use of usually wasted space under the stairs.*

A combination of drawers and cupboards, open shelves and ones with doors offers the most flexibility. Shown here, from top to bottom: A beautifully crafted, pale sage green built-in storage unit has deeper, closed storage up to counter height and shallower shelves and cupboards above. In a mud room at the back door, a wall of open shelves combined with a chest of drawers topped by a corkboard provides storage of all kinds.

Design

FRONT MATTER

1: Molly English/Camps and Cottages; **2:** Design: Karen and Shaun Burke/Bravura Finishes Decorative Painting; **4 top:** Design: Molly English/Camps and Cottages; **4 middle:** Interior design: Kendall Wilkinson Design; **4 bottom:** Design: Jane Walter and Robert Adams/SummerHouse; **5 top right:** Interior design: Gigi Rogers Designs, www.gigirogersdesigns.com; **5 middle right:** Interior designer: John D. Oetgen; **5 bottom right:** Interior design: McWhorter/Ross Design Group, www.mcwhorterdesign.com.

DECORATING BASICS

6–7: Interior designer: Paulette Trainor; **8–9:** Interior design: Gail Lesley Diehl Interiors; **10:** Nancy Gilbert/San Anselmo Country Store; **11 top:** Interior designer: Frank Van Duerm Design Associates; **11 bottom:** Decorative painter: James Allen Smith; Interior design: Gary Crain; **12 bottom:** Denise Balaser; **13:** Design: Nancy Gilbert/San Anselmo Country Store; **14:** Lighting designer: Linda Ferry; Interior designer: Edward Perrault Design Associates, Inc.; **15 top:** Designer: David Smith; **15 bottom:** Interior designer: Dominique Sanchot Stenzel—La Belle France; Decorative painter: The Master's Touch; Builder: Godby Construction, Inc.; **16:** Designer: Rosmari Agostini; Stylist: Mary Jane Ryburn; **17:** Interior designer: Katherine Hill Interiors; **18:** Mark Bartos of Hortus Garden/Design; **20 top:** Architect: James McCalligan; **20 bottom:** Interior designer: EJ Interior Design; **21:** Design: Christine Worboys; **22 top:** Decorative artist: Shelly Masters Decorative Painting; Interior designer: Paulette Trainor; **22 bottom:** Interior designer: Tucker & Marks; Architects: Hunt, Hale & Associates; Contractor: Kelly Pacific; Decorative painter: Page Kelleher; **23 top:** Interior design: Victoria Lohse/Korb Interiors, www.design4thepassionate.com; **23 bottom:** Design: Courtyard Collection; **24 top:** Interior design: McWhorter/Ross Design Group, www.mcwhorterdesign.com; **25:** Architects: Hsin-Ming Fung and Craig Hodgetts; **26:** Interior design: Joan Osburn/Osburn Design; **28 top:** Design: Michael Walters; **28 bottom:** Designer: Deborah Leamann Interiors; **29:** Design: Courtyard Collection; **30 left:** Design: Summer House at One Ford Road, Newport Beach, by Pacific Bay Homes; **30 right:** Eugenia Erskine Jesberg/EJ Interior Design, www.ejinteriordesign.com; **31:** Interior designer: Dominique Sanchot Stenzel—La Belle France; Builder: Godby Construction, Inc.; **32:** Interior designer: Ruth Livingston Interior Design; **33 top:** Design: Summer House at One Ford Road, Newport Beach, by Pacific Bay Homes; **33 bottom:** Architect and Interior designer: Stephen W. Sanborn; **34 top:** Interior designer: Lindsay Steenblock/County Clare Design; **34 bottom:** Interior Design: Paulette Trainor/Trainor and Associates Design; **35:** Interior designer: Richard Witzel & Associates; **36:** Designer/decorative painter: Peggy Del Rosario; **37 top:** Interior design: Kimberly Lamer Interiors and Sandra Lamer Interiors; **37 bottom:** Interior design: Karen Graul; Kitchen design: Kirk Craig; Architect: Kurt Archer; **38:** Interior design: Osburn Design; **40:** Architect: Alla Kazovsky/Kids' Studio; **41 top:** Interior designer: Osburn Design; **41 bottom:** Interior design: Gigi Rogers Designs, www.gigirogersdesigns.com; **42 top:** Interior designer: Sasha Emerson Design Studio; **42 bottom:** Interior designer: City Studios; **43:** Interior designer: City Studios/Sienna Pacific; **45 top:** Interior designer: City Studios; **45 bottom:** Interior designer: Sasha Emerson Levin; **46:** Interior designer: Bauer Interior Design; **47 top:** Interior designer: Cathleen Waronker and Melissa Dietz with "Little Folk Art"; **47 bottom:** Interior designer: Osburn Design; Architect: Louis Butler/Butler Armsden Architects; **48 both:** "idea house" at San Francisco Design Center; **49:** "idea house" at San Francisco Design Center; **50 top:** Design: Kit Parmentier/Allison Rose; **50 middle:** Decorative painter: Carla Eagleton/Trump; Interior design: Sudie Woodson Interiors; **50 bottom:** Design: Brad Polvorosa; **51 top:** Decorative artist: Page Kelleher; **51 middle:** Interior Design: City Studios; **51 bottom:** Interior designer: Elizabeth Hill/Selby House Ltd.; Window treatment: Rossetti & Corriea Draperies; **52 top:** Architect: House + House of San Francisco; Interior design: Osburn Design; **52 middle:** Interior designer: Carol A. Spong; Colorist: Mary Beth Burnham; **52 bottom:** Design: Molly English/Camps and Cottages; **53 top:** "idea house" at San Francisco Design Center; **53 middle:** Interior designer: Kendall Wilkinson Design; **53 bottom:** Architect: Charles Debbas; Contractor: Kevin Reimer/The Builder Group; **54 right:** Decorative artist: Studio Roshambeau; **55 left:** Design: Malibu Ceramic Works; **55 right:** Architect: Richard Crandall; Light fixtures and art glass: Mark Rubnitz/ATOMIC GLASS; General contractor: Jonejan/Schaadt Construction; **56 top:** Interior designers: Katherine Murray and Suzanne Ferrari/Ta da! design in a day; **56 bottom:** Interior designer: Nestor D. Matthews/Matthews Studio; **58:** Interior designer: Lisa DeLong/DeLong Designs & Interiors; Decorative painter: Carla Eagleton/Trump; **59 top:** Architectural design: Andre Rothblatt; **59 bottom:** Interior design: Richard Witzel & Associates; **60:** Interior design: Richard Witzel & Associates; **62 top:** Architect: Remick Associates Architects-Builders, Inc.; Tile: Stonelight Tile Company; **62 bottom:** Interior designer: Kendall Wilkinson Design; **63:** Design: Jane Walter and Robert Adams/SummerHouse; **64:** Interior designer: John D. Oetgen; **65:** Interior designer: Kit Parmentier/Allison Rose; **66 top:** "idea house" at San Francisco Design Center; **66 bottom:** Interior design: Tres McKinney/Richard Witzel & Associates; **67:** Interior design: Bonis-Mariotti & Associates; **68 top:** "idea house" at San Francisco Design Center; **68 bottom:** Architect: James McCalligan; **69:** Interior design: Pacific Dimensions, Inc.; Architect: Bassenian/Lagoni Architects; **70 top:** "idea house" at San Francisco Design Center; Decorative artist: Erik Seniska; **70 bottom:** Interior designer: Sandra Tofanelli-Gordon; **71 top right:** "idea house" at San Francisco Design Center; **71 middle right:** Design: Laura Taylor Moore/Interior Services of Los Gatos and Betty Benesi/Cottage Industries; Stencil: Jonathan Davis; **71 middle left:** Design: Taylor Woodrow; **71 bottom right:** Design: Michael Muha of M.G. Michael & Associates, Inc.

PLANNING PRIMER

72–73: Interior design: Dianne Adams; Window treatment: Mary's Custom Workroom; **74:** Interior design: Kendall Wilkinson Design; **76:** Interior design: Tres McKinney/Laura Ashley; **77 left:** Interior design: Gigi Rogers Designs, www.gigirogersdesigns.com; **79:** Stylist: Julie Atwood; **80 top:** Design: Dovetail Design; **81:** Design: Layne Gray; **83 top left:** Cushion design: Dale Miller; **83 top right:** Interior design: Gigi Rogers Designs, www.gigirogersdesigns.com; **83 middle left:** Interior designer: Alison Lufkin/Sullivan & Company; **83 middle right:** Interior designer: Cathleen Waronker and Melissa Dietz; **83 bottom left:** Design: Nancy Bostwick/Nancy's Maison et Jardin Antiques; **83 bottom right:** Interior designer: Kelly A. London and Deborah A. London; **84 top:** Interior design: Kathryne Designs; **85:** Interior design: Sasha Emerson Design Studio; **87:** Interior designer: Mel Lowrance; **88:** Architectural design: Steven Goldstein; **90:** Interior designer: Kendall Wilkinson Design; **91 top:** Interior designer: Kit Parmentier/Allison Rose; **91 bottom:** Decorative painter: Robert O'Conner Designs; **92 left:** Designer/decorative painter: Peggy Del Rosario; **92 right:** Decorative painter: Gail Leddy; **93 top left:** Decorative painter: Justina Jorrin Barnard; **93 top right:** Interior design: Michael Lane; **93 middle right:** Decorative painter: Justina Jorrin Barnard; **93 bottom left:** Interior design: Charles Spada; **96 left:** Interior design: Melissa Griggs Interior Design; **96 right:** Design: Taylor Woodrow; **97 top:** Design: Pamela Green Interiors; **97 bottom:** Design: Mary McWilliams; **98:** Interior design: Shirley Jensen/Forget-Me-Nots Designs; Architectural design: Michael Bolton; Construction: Dru Jensen; Decorative painting: Jolene Howell; **100 left:** Interior designer: Osburn Design; **100 right:** Decorative painter: Erik Seniska; **101:** "idea house" at San Francisco Design Center; **102 top:** Architect: Robert Remiker; Interior design: Sarita Patel; Landscape design: Angela and Tom Campbell; **103 top:** "idea house" at San Francisco Design Center; **103 bottom:** Design: Lee Najman; **107:** Interior designer: Jay Jeffers/Richard Witzel & Associates; **108:**

Interior designer: Suzanne Tucker/Tucker & Marks; Architects: Hunt, Hale & Associates; **109:** Interior designer: Kathryne Dahlman/ Kathryne Designs; **110:** Interior designer: Monty Collins and Willem Racké; **111 top:** Design: Summer House at One Ford Road, Newport Beach, by Pacific Bay Homes; **111 bottom:** Interior designer: George Davis Interiors; **112:** Interior designer: Tres McKinney/Laura Ashley; **113 top:** smith+noble windoware; **113 bottom:** Design: Summer House at One Ford Road, Newport Beach, by Pacific Bay Homes; **114 right:** smith+noble windoware; **114 left:** Interior designer: Elizabeth Hill of Selby House Ltd.; Window treatment: Rossetti & Corriea Draperies; **121 bottom:** Interior design: Trish Dietze; Floral design: Tom Stokey; Garden design: Trish Dietze, Randy Bommarito, and Joye Long; **122 left:** Interior designer: Kathryne Dahlman/Kathryne Designs; **122 right:** Interior design: Osburn Design; **123 top:** Design: Eileen Boyd Design; **128 top:** Interior design: Molly McGowan Interiors; Cabinetry: Rutt of Lafayette, www.ruttoflafayette.com; **129 right:** Interior design: David Ramey/David Ramey Interior Design; **130 bottom:** Design: Minor Revisions Architecture & Design; Contractor: Mark McCarthy; Tile: Buddy Rhodes Studio/Amalfi Tile & Marble; **132:** Interior design and lighting: Margaret M. Wimmer; Architect: Carrasco & Associates; **134 left:** Architect: Remick Associates Architects-Builders, Inc.; Interior designer: Gary Hutton Designs; **134 right:** Lighting designer: Catherine Ng/Lightsmiths Design Group; Interior designer: Judith Owen Interiors; Custom home builder: The Owen Companies; **135:** Lighting designer: Catherine Ng/Lightsmiths Design Group; Architect: The Bradley Group; Designer: Eckhard Evers; **136 bottom:** Lighting designer: Linda Ferry; Architect: Eric Miller Architects, Inc.; Glass artist: Ahnalisa Miller; **137:** Design: Scott Design—Interior Architecture & Design and Epifanio Juarez (Juarez Design); **138:** Interior design: Kathy Coomer/Art Pie and Daniel Daniloff/Design Changes; **140 left:** Interior design: Jean Horn Interiors; **140 right:** Lighting designer: Linda Ferry; Architect: Charles Rose; Glass artist: Masaoka Glass Design; **141:** Interior designer: Stephen W. Sanborn; **142 top:** Architect: Jane Mah; Contractor: Steven Donaldson; **142 bottom:** Interior designer: Osburn Design; **143:** Lighting designer: Bryan Burkhart/California Architectural Lighting; **144:** Lighting designer: Linda Ferry; Architect: Charles Rose; General contractor: Dennis Jones; **145:** Architect: Morimoto Architects.

GREAT IDEAS

146–147: Interior designer: Lindsay Steenblock/County Clare Design; Architect: Robert Earl; **148:** Interior design: Frank Van Duerm Design Associates; **150:** Architectural design: Steven Goldstein; **151 top:** Interior design: Elizabeth Hill/Selby House Ltd.; **151 bottom:** Interior design: Tucker & Marks, Inc., www.tuckerandmarks.com; **152:** Interior design: Kathleen Navarra/Navarra Design Consultants; **153:** Interior design: Molly McGowan Interiors; Cabinetry: Rutt of Lafayette, www.ruttoflafayette.com; **154:** Interior designer: Richard Witzel/Richard Witzel & Associates; **155 top:** Interior design: Kimberly Lamer Interiors and Sandra Lamer Interiors; **155 bottom:** Interior design: Kendall Wilkinson Design; **157 top:** Interior designer: Kathryne Dahlman/Kathryne Designs; **157 bottom:** Design: Jane Walter and Robert Adams/SummerHouse; **159:** Interior design: Jeff Shuler/Jeff Shuler & Associates; **160 top right:** Design: Nancy Bostwick/Nancy's Maison et Jardin Antiques; **160 middle right:** Designer: Rosmari Agostini; Stylist: Mary Jane Ryburn; **161 bottom:** Interior design: Kendall Wilkinson Design; **162:** Design: Richard Witzel & Associates; **164 left:** Interior designer: Richard Witzel & Associates; **165:** Interior design: Monty Collins Interior Design; **166 top:** Decorative painter: Samantha Renko Decorative Arts Studio; **166 bottom:** Interior designer: Linda Applewhite; **167:** Design: Nancy Bostwick/Nancy's Maison et Jardin Antiques; **168:** Design: Dovetail Design; **169 top:** Interior designer: Carol S. Shawn; **169 bottom:** Interior design: Denise Foley Design and David Brewster; **170:** Interior design: Jennifer Bevan Interiors; **172:** Interior design: David Dalton Associates, Inc.; **173 top:** Design: Richard Witzel & Associates; **173**

bottom: Design: Sandra C. Watkins; Paint color and fabrics: Joan Osburn/Osburn Design, www.osburndesign.com; Paint: Mark McMahon and Mark Dillon/Chameleon Fine Painting; Office unit and shelving: Thomas World Furniture Design and Fabrication; **174:** Interior design: Eugenia Erskine Jesberg/EJ Interior Design, www.ejinteriordesign.com; **176:** Interior designer: Agnes Bourne, Inc.; **177 bottom:** Janice Stone Thomas/Stone•Wood Design, Inc.; **178 top:** Design: David & Vicki Ritter; Builder: David Ritter Construction; **178 bottom:** Interior designer: Macfee & Associates Interior Design; **179:** Interior designer: Lou Ann Bauer; **180:** Interior designer: Lisa DeLong/DeLong Designs & Interiors; **181:** Interior designer: Rick Sambol; **182:** Architectural and interior designer: Lynn Hollyn; **183 top:** Interior design: Molly McGowan Interiors; Cabinetry: Rutt of Lafayette, www.ruttoflafayette.com; **183 bottom:** Design: Taylor Woodrow; **184:** Design: Kelly A. London and Deborah A. London; Architect: Rushton-Chartock Architects; **185 top:** Design: Christine Worboys; **185 bottom:** Design/contractor: City Building, Inc.; **186:** Architect: Dennis O'Conner/The O'Conner Company; Landscape architect: Marta Fry Landscape; Interior design: Elizabeth Hill/Selby House Ltd.; **188 left:** Interior design: Elizabeth Hill/Selby House Ltd.; **188 right:** Interior design: Surrey Interiors; Architect: J. Allen Sayles; Contractor: Da Silva Construction, Inc.; **189:** Interior design: Trish Dietze; Floral design: Tom Stokey; Garden design: Trish Dietze, Randy Bommarito, and Joye Long; **190 top:** Design: Summer House at One Ford Road, Newport Beach, by Pacific Bay Homes; **190 bottom:** Interior design: Lorenzo Petroni and Maria Elena Petroni Interiors; Architect: James McCalligan; **191:** Interior design: Claudia Fleury/ Claudia's Designs; **192:** Interior design: D. Kimberly Smith/Deer Creek Design; **193:** Interior design: David Dalton Associates, Inc.; **194 top:** Interior design: Sandy Bacon/Sandy Bacon Design Group; Home theater: John Maxon/Integrated System Design; Cabinets: Heartwood Studio; **194 bottom:** Interior design: Amanda Knobel and Linda Miller/Renaissance Interior Design; **195:** Interior design: Jeff Shuler/Jeff Shuler & Associates; **196 top left:** Design: Paul Zsafen; **196 top right:** Architect: Karl Golden; **196 bottom right:** Design: Nancy Gilbert/San Anselmo Country Store; **197 top left:** Design: Jane Walter and Robert Adams/SummerHouse; **197 bottom left:** Interior designer: Bauer Interior Design; Tile: Elle Terry Leonard/ Architectural Ceramics; **197 bottom right:** Interior designer: Thomas Bartlett Interiors; Tile: Elle Terry Leonard/Architectural Ceramics; **198:** Architect: Bassenian/Lagoni Architects; Interior design: Pacific Dimensions, Inc.; **201 top:** Design: John Gillespie; **201 bottom:** Interior design: Melissa Griggs; Architectural design: Bill Galli, www.wdgalli.com; **202:** Architect: James McCalligan; **203:** Interior design: Pacific Dimensions, Inc.; Architect: Bassenian/Lagoni Architects; **204:** Architect: Dan Nelson/Designs Northwest Architects; **205 top:** Cabinets: Kevin Coy; Contractor/Builder: Peter Kyle; **205 bottom:** Interior design: Donald Clement and Bob Powers; Architect: Donald Clement and Jim McCalligan; **206:** Design: Markie Nelson Interior Design; **207:** Design: Creative Design Consultants; Architect: Schuerer Architects; **208:** Interior design: Barbara Jacobs; Cabinetry fabrication: Dana Karren; **209:** Design: Lisa Malloy/Interior Inspirations; **210:** Interior design: D. Kimberly Smith/Deer Creek Design; **213 top:** Lighting designer: Becca Foster Lighting Design; Architect: Michael Harris Architecture; Contractor: Peter Moffat Construction; **213 bottom:** Architect and Interior design: J. Reed Robbins; **215:** Design: J. Reed Robbins; Antique accessories: Lottie Ballou Classic Clothing; **216:** Design: Jane Walter and Robert Adams/ SummerHouse; **217 top:** Interior design: Kit Parmentier/Allison Rose; **217 bottom:** Interior design: Elizabeth Hill/Selby House Ltd.; **218 left:** "idea house" at San Francisco Design Center; **218 right:** Interior design: Amy Devault, assisted by Kira Taylor and Lynn Klopfenstein/Amy Devault Interior Design; **219 left:** "idea house" at San Francisco Design Center; **219 right:** Interior design: Tres McKinney/Laura Ashley; **220 top:** Design: Nancy Bostwick/Nancy's Maison et Jardin Antiques; **220 bottom:** Interior design: Gigi Rogers Designs, www.gigirogersdesigns.com; **221:** Design: Molly

English/Camps and Cottages; Sign design: Steve Reed; **222:** Interior design: Norm Claybaugh/Juvenile Lifestyles, Inc.; Muralist: Debbra; **224 bottom:** Interior design: Norm Claybaugh/Juvenile Lifestyles Inc.; **225:** Interior design: Kathleen Navarra/ Navarra Design Consultants; **226:** Artist: Catherine Richards; **227 top:** Decorative painting: Deborah Disman/The Artifactory Studio; **227 bottom:** Interior design: Elizabeth Benefield; **228:** Design: Linda Woodrum; **229 top:** Stenciling: Susan Griffin; **229 bottom:** Interior design: Barbara McQueen Interior Design; **230:** Interior design: Norm Claybaugh/Juvenile Lifestyles, Inc.; Muralist: Debbra; **231 top:** Decorative painter: James Hartman; **231 bottom:** Muralist: Demar Feldman Studios/Miriam Feldman; Furniture from Imagine That; **232 top left:** Interior design: Sasha Emerson Design Studio; **232 top right:** Interior design: Molly McGowan Interiors; Cabinetry: Rutt of Lafayette, www.ruttoflafayette.com; **232 middle right:** Interior design: Janice Olsen/JD-Just Design by Janice; **232 bottom right:** Interior design: David Dalton Associates, Inc.; **233 all:** Interior design: Norm Claybaugh/Juvenile Lifestyles, Inc.; **234:** Design: Fu-Tung Cheng/Cheng Design; **236:** Interior design: Jeanese Rowell Design, www.jrdesign.com; **237 top:** Design: Cia Foreman; Contractor: Ron Middel; **237 bottom:** Architect: Backen, Arragoni & Ross; **238 top:** Interior designer: Bauer Interior Design; **238 bottom:** Design: Karen and Shaun Burke/Bravura Finishes Decorative Painting; **240:** Interior designer: Paul Vincent Wiseman; **241:** Architect: Remick Associates Architects-Builders, Inc.; **242:** Design: Melanie Born; **244:** Design: Jarvis Architects; **246 left:** Interior design: Marc Reusser and Debra Bergstrom/Reusser Bergstrom Associates, www.rbadesign.com; **246 right:** Interior design: Carolyn E. Oliver-Broder/Oliver's Interiors and Antiques, www.oliverinteriors.com; Decorative painting: Loretta Weeks; **247:** Interior designer: Agins Interiors; **248:** Interior design: Alison Lufkin/Sullivan & Company; **249 top:** Interior design: Shirley Jensen/Forget-Me-Nots Designs; Architectural design: Michael Bolton; Construction: Dru Jensen; Decorative painting: Jolene Howell; **249 bottom:** Design: Christine Worboys; **250:** Interior design: Molly McGowan Interiors; Cabinetry: Rutt of Lafayette, www.ruttoflafayette.com; **251 top:** Architectural design: Jarvis Architects; **251 bottom:** Design: Dan Phipps & Associates Architects; Cabinets: Detail A Studios; **252 top left:** Interior designer: Elizabeth Hill/Selby House Ltd.; **252 top right:** Interior design: Debi Cekosh/Cekosh Design Studio; Architectural design: Michael Gibson; **252 bottom right:** Interior design: S.E.A. Design/Build; **253 top left:** Design: Janine Liddle/A Room with a View; **253 bottom left:** Interior designer: Ann Davies Interiors; **253 right:** Interior designer: Geoffrey De Sousa/de sousa hughes; **254:** Interior designer: Susan Federman/Federman, Johnston; **256:** Interior design: Kathryne Designs; **257:** Interior designer: Paulette Trainor; **259 top:** Design: Jane Walter and Robert Adams/SummerHouse; **259 bottom:** Interior design: Michael D. Trapp; **260:** Interior design: Osburn Design; **261:** Interior design: Thomas Bartlett Interiors of Napa; **262:** Design: Karen and Shaun Burke/Bravura Finishes Decorative Painting; **264 top:** Designers: Jenny and Peter Venegas; **264 bottom:** Design: Christine Worboys; **265:** Architect: Bokal & Sneed Architects; **266 top:** Design: Velda E. Newman; General Contractor: Buddy G. Newman; **266 bottom:** Architect: Robert Wylie; **268 top left:** Interior design: Kathryne Dahlman and Meg Carper/Kathryne Designs; **268 top right:** Architectural and interior design: Pamela Dreyfuss Interior Design; Millwork and doors: Creative Cabinets; **268 bottom right:** Courtyard design: Carlos Mora; Garden design: Yvonne Axene assisted by Saul Velsquez; **269 left:** Design: Artistic Botanical Creations; **269 right:** Design: Carl & Tiffany Ledbetter, Jon Courter/Courter Construction; **270:** Interior design: Patricia Symes and Associates; **272:** Design: Molly English/Camps and Cottages; **273:** Architect: Steven Goldstein; **274:** Architect: Mark Becker, Inc.; **275 top:** Interior designer: Claudia Fleury/Claudia's Designs; **275 bottom:** Architect: Jarvis Architects; **277 top:** Architect: Ted Wengren; **277 bottom:** Architect: Mark Horton; **278 left:** Interior designer: Stephen W. Sanborn; **278 top right:** Design and fabrication of changing units: Paul La Bruna; Stenciling: Susan Griffin; **278 bottom right:** Design: Jacobson, Silverstein & Winslow Architects/Paul Winans Construction, Inc.; **279 top:** Donham & Sweeny Architects; **279 bottom:** Architect/designer: Donald Clement;

Cabinet fabrication: Apple Woodworks; **280 top:** Architect: Edward Buchanan/Jarvis Architects; **280 bottom:** Interior design: Wayne Palmer; **281 bottom:** Interior design: Timothy Guetzlaff/ TMG + Associates; **282 top left:** Timothy Guetzlaff/TMG + Associates; **282 top right:** Kevin Patrick O'Brien & Janice Stone Thomas; **282 bottom right:** Ronald W. Madson/Madson Associates; **283 top:** Construction: Tom Hampson; **283 bottom:** Interior design: Lisa Malloy/Interior Inspirations.

Photography

American Olean: 102 bottom; **Armstrong World Industries, Inc.:** 126 bottom, 127 top; **Blackstock Leather, Inc.:** 130 top; **Antoine Bootz:** 5 middle right, 64; **Bruce Hardwood Floors:** 120, 121 top, 164 right, 212, 214; **Congoleum Corporation:** 124 both; **Phillip Ennis:** 11 bottom, 12 bottom, 67; **Forbo Linoleum, Inc.:** 125, 118; **Formica Corporation:** 126 top, 127 bottom; **Tria Giovan:** 92 right, 161 top; **John Granen:** 206; **Ken Gutmaker:** 57, 59 top, 83 middle left, 88, 96 left, 98, 138, 150, 151 bottom, 160 top left, 166 bottom, 201 bottom, 233 bottom, 248, 249 top, 251 top, 252 bottom right, 275 top; **Jamie Hadley:** 1, 2, 3, 4 all, 5 top right and bottom right, 8, 10, 13, 21, 23 top, 24 top, 26, 41 bottom, 42 top, 50 top, 52 bottom, 63, 65, 74, 77 left, 83 bottom left, 85, 91 top, 97 top, 102 top, 109, 115 left, 121 bottom, 122 left, 129 right, 136 top, 140 left, 157 both, 160 top right, 167, 173 bottom, 185 top, 189, 196 top right and bottom right, 197 top left, 207, 208, 209, 216, 217 top, 220–221 all, 224 top, 225, 232 top left, 238 bottom, 244, 249 bottom, 259 both, 262, 264 bottom, 266 top, 268 top right and bottom right, 270, 272, 273, 274, 275 bottom, 277 bottom, 279 bottom, 280 top, 281 bottom, 282 top left, 283 bottom; **Margot Hartford:** 282 bottom right; **Philip Harvey:** 14, 18, 23 bottom, 28 top, 29, 32, 33 bottom, 36, 47 bottom, 50 bottom, 52 top, 53 bottom, 55 left, 56 both, 62 top, 71 middle left and middle right, 92 left, 96 right, 100 left, 122 right, 130 bottom, 132, 134 both, 135, 136 bottom, 137, 140 right, 141, 142 bottom, 143, 144, 145, 169 top, 170, 172, 176, 177 bottom, 179, 181, 182, 183 bottom, 185 bottom, 193, 197 bottom left and bottom right, 202, 213 both, 215, 237 both, 238 top, 240, 241, 243, 260, 261, 265, 266 bottom, 269 both, 278 left and bottom right; **Alex Hayden:** 204; **Greg Hursley/Through the Lens:** 24 bottom; **Dennis Krukowski:** 93 top right; **Barry Lewis:** 16, 160 middle right; **Jane Lidz:** 242; **davidduncanlivingston.com:** 158, 178 bottom, 239; **Sylvia Martin:** 97 bottom, 228; **Masland Carpets and Rugs:** 129 left; **Steven Mays:** 93 top left and middle right; **E. Andrew McKinney:** 6–7, 11 top, 15 bottom, 17, 20 both, 22 both, 30–31 all, 33 top, 34–35 all, 37 top, 38, 40, 41 top, 42 bottom, 43, 45 both, 46, 47 top, 48–49 all, 50 middle, 51 all, 52 middle, 53 top and middle, 54 right, 55 right, 58, 59 bottom, 60, 62 bottom, 66 both, 68 both, 69, 70 both, 71 top right, 72–73, 76, 77 right, 80–81 all, 83 top left, top right, middle right, bottom right, 84 bottom, 87, 90, 91 bottom, 100 right, 101, 103 top, 107, 108, 110, 111 both, 112, 113 both, 114 both, 115 right, 128 both, 142 top, 146–147, 148, 151 top, 152, 153, 154–155 all, 159, 160 bottom right, 161 bottom, 162, 164 left, 165, 166 top, 168, 169 bottom, 173 top, 174, 178 top, 180, 183 top, 184, 186, 188 both, 190–191 all, 192, 194 top,195, 198, 200, 203, 205 both, 210, 217 bottom, 218–219 all, 222, 224 bottom, 226–227 all, 229 both, 230, 231 bottom, 232 top right, middle right, and bottom right, 233 top, 234, 236, 246–247 all, 250, 252 top left, 253 all, 254, 257, 264 top, 267, 268 top left, 278 top right, 283 top; **Melabee M. Miller:** 28 bottom; **Emily Minton:** 37 bottom; **Bradley Olman:** 93 middle left; **Tom Rider:** 79; **Eric Roth:** 93 bottom left; **Mark Samu:** 103 bottom,123 bottom; **Alan Shortall:** 19, 123 top; **Brad Simmons/beateworks.com:** 12 top, 156, 258; **Michael Skott:** 84 top, 94, 104, 252 top right, 256, 276; **smith+noble windoware:** 106; **SPC Photo Collection:** 194 bottom; **Tim Street-Porter:** 25, 54, left; **Tim Street-Porter/beateworks.com:** 196 top left, 281 top; **John Sutton:** 251 bottom; **Brian Vanden Brink:** 201 top, 277 top, 279 top; **David Wakely:** 231 top, 280 bottom, 282 top right; **Jessie Walker Associates:** 15 top, 71 bottom right; **Wicanders Cork Flooring:** 5 bottom left, 71 bottom left, 171, 177 top.

Index